PRAISE FOR

THE **RELEVANCE** PATH

"I have worked with Marcy Eisenberg for almost ten years. She has the uncanny ability to engage with the customer and navigate through incredibly complicated projects with agility and tact rarely seen in the government contracting sector. Her ability to bring RELEVANCE to a new project, or rescue a failing project, is the culmination of both passion and vision written into this unique methodology. I highly recommend that anyone looking to begin a new venture or fix a broken process read this book."

—Adam Hicks
Information Security Manager, Feed the Children

"I have known Marcy Eisenberg for ten-plus years. Having been in the technical services industry for over forty-four years it refreshing to see an executive who does not live by ninety-day Wall Street cycles, but rather who takes the long view focusing on complete client satisfaction and all facets of employee welfare. The 'right thing' is almost always found by taking the high road. Marcy is an excellent navigator along that road."

—Pete Hatfield
Current executive at AECOM and former executive at
Digital Equipment Corporation, Cray Research, Northrop Grumman

"A workplace environment should inspire superior employee commitment, morale, and performance. As much as companies talk about accountability, leaders seldom understand what practical steps to take to achieve an ethic of service that makes accountability meaningful and rewarding. Educating citizen soldiers, protecting and serving our community, and ultimately doing the right thing is what shapes Norwich University's approach to business and mission in higher education. The Relevance Path™ exemplifies the way forward for those who seek a proven road map for success. This is a must-read for serious leaders!"

—Richard W. Schneider

RADM, USCGR (Ret.); President, Norwich University

"Marcy Eisenberg's deep experience in the national security field gives her a unique insight into the inner workings of our government's contracting system and how to achieve the best results as a contractor. Marcy clearly lays out the fundamentals of how to work with clients and understand their thought processes, limitations, and depths of knowledge to create win-win solutions for everyone. In my experience, Marcy and her staff live by the lessons she teaches in this book, which makes Pathoras an excellent partner in any project."

—Sohan V. Mikkilineni

Managing partner, General Technology Systems LLC

"Marcy and Pathoras have created the cookbook for efficient project creation. I would recommend this book to anyone that needs to stay on target in a complex environment."

—Matthew Creedican

Former US Navy SEAL; CEO, Verivis LLC

"Eisenberg's work represents some of the most imaginative, innovative, insightful experiences and provided wisdom that I've gotten my hands on and brain around in a very long while. The application of her work in this book is unlimited, with results near immeasurable and absolutely invaluable to the reader/pursuer. What a great find!"

—David P. Fridovich

Lieutenant general (Ret.), United States Army, former commanding general, Special Operations command, Pacific, and deputy commander, United States Special Operations command

THE RELEVANCE PATH™

THE RELEVANCE PATH™

7 STEPS TO
GIVE YOUR
ORGANIZATION
A DECISIVE EDGE

MARCY EISENBERG

Published by Advantage, Charleston, South Carolina.
Member of Advantage Media Group.

ADVANTAGE is a registered trademark, and the Advantage colophon is a trademark of Advantage Media Group, Inc.

Printed in the United States of America.

10 9 8 7 6 5 4 3 2 1

ISBN: 978-1-59932-735-8
LCCN: 2020907388

Cover design by Carly Blake.
Layout design by Wesley Strickland.

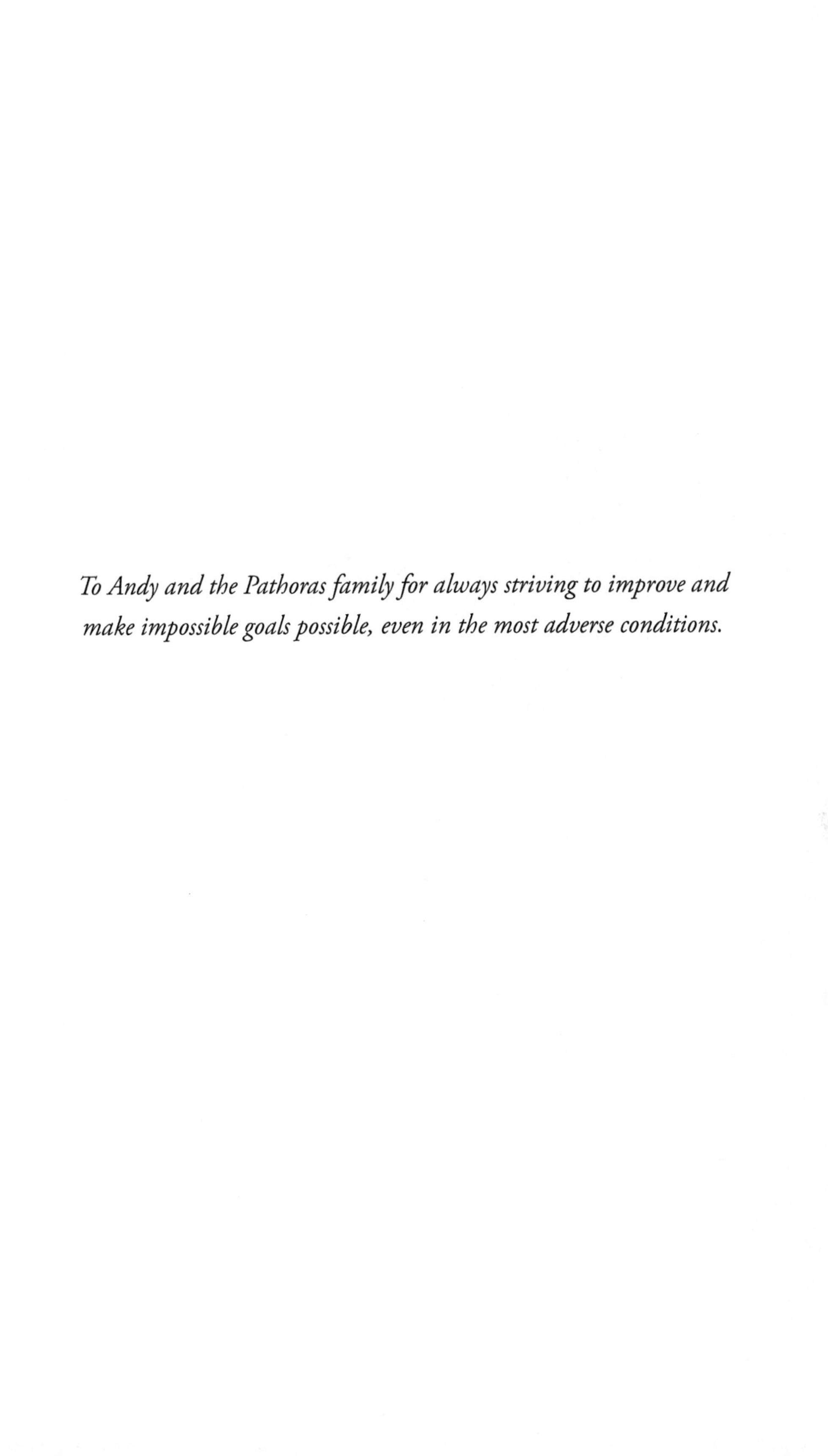

To Andy and the Pathoras family for always striving to improve and make impossible goals possible, even in the most adverse conditions.

CONTENTS

FOREWORD

By Steve Spano, Brigadier General (Ret.), US Air Force

I first met Marcy when I retired from the Air Force and entered the corporate world in 2011. She and her husband, Andrew, were in the early years of building Pathoras. It didn't take long into our first breakfast meeting to be impressed with their passion, dreams, and determination to work as a team to make Pathoras relevant. Together, Marcy and Andrew built a highly talented team and proceeded to execute a patient but persistent strategy. Their business growth and success has yielded several eye-opening accolades, and they are just getting started.

Pathoras's success alone wasn't unique. Many startups began the same way Pathoras launched. In fact, many who read this might feel they are already doing most or all of the seven steps outlined in this book. However, it isn't just about "doing the steps" that lead to RELEVANCE. Pathoras achieved RELEVANCE by integrating and executing the seven steps with laser-like precision. More importantly, they successfully baked them into the fabric of their corporate culture. The seven steps to RELEVANCE isn't an instruction guide or checklist. The secret sauce is in how Pathoras executed and made it a philosophy that is turning into a movement. After several enlightening discussions over the years about their strategy, leadership, family, and even wine, I realized Marcy and Andrew had to share their story with the rest of the world.

Each step of this book, taken alone, may come across to the casual observer as just good common sense business practice. I'll admit at first blush I fell into the same trap. I've seen many new processes and programs in my Air Force career that either failed to meet objectives or were simply quietly abandoned because they were too difficult to scale and institutionalize. More often in my experience these good ideas and programs fell apart due to their complexity and lack of disciplined execution. However, Pathoras sidestepped these pitfalls, and the results are transformative.

The true awakening for me emerged with clarity when I recognized how each step, while functioning as a stand-alone process, was inextricably linked to each of the previous steps. Precise execution created a cumulative and powerful momentum, which, by the conclusion of step seven, resulted in an epic crescendo that is driving a growing gap between many good organizations and the more relevant ones like Pathoras.

While RELEVANCE was designed to help businesses, by their very nature the seven steps can apply to your daily life. Who doesn't feel personal challenges or relationships can be more relevant through such things as better engagement and listening, communicating in more effective ways, or executing on personal goals? The beauty of RELEVANCE is that is it relevant to every business and every young or older adult.

Transformation is really about being relevant in periods of disruption. Every business and every individual will face a number of disruptions throughout their existence. Along the way there are numerous avenues to seek help. Many often yield significant and positive results. However, for the vast majority of businesses (or individuals) interested in breaking from the pack, RELEVANCE is a true game changer.

ACKNOWLEDGMENTS

Thank you, Andy—my husband, and partner in life and Pathoras—for always believing in me, inspiring me, and supporting me in building RELEVANCE. You are without doubt the best friend I could have never even imagined becoming a part of my life, and you make me a better wife, friend, and mother. I have loved all of our adventures together and am so excited for what the future brings for us and our boys.

Thank you to Scott, for supporting me in this endeavor, no matter how crazy it sounded at times. And for how crazy I may have sounded over these many years at Pathoras.

Thank you to my parents, Linda and Ed, and in-laws, Judy and Tom, for always helping—and humoring—me as I spent countless hours consumed while pushing forward with this book (and as you tirelessly cared for our family's needs when I couldn't). You are without a doubt the most supportive and caring sets of parents Andy and I could have ever dreamed of.

Thank you to Sarah, Tammy, Preston, Kristi, Justin, Alissa, JP, and Steve, for being sounding boards as we refined RELEVANCE. The Relevance Path would not be what it is today without your keen eyes and expertise at Pathoras.

Thank you to Pete for remaining a true friend, mentor, advisor, and confidant in all personal and professional matters.

Thank you to Frido, Matt, Sohan, Bob, Adam, and President Schneider for always being great supporters and partners to Pathoras. We're grateful for our friendships and relationships with each of you, as well as growing our partnerships out in the future.

I would also like to acknowledge the many talented personnel who have dedicated their lives to protecting our national security. Many of these talented individuals cannot be openly acknowledged in this book for security reasons, but they have been more than generous in acknowledging the many successes RELEVANCE has provided them.

INTRODUCTION

The Seven Steps of RELEVANCE: Giving Your Organization a Decisive Edge and Making Your Project Goals a Reality

Happiness, success, and excellence, they are not something you get from knowing the path. They are something you experience by walking it.

—Steve Mariboli

I learned long ago that making projects relevant is what gives any team, organization, or objective a decisive edge over a mission, the competition, or adversaries.

For years, my company, Pathoras, and I have seen firsthand projects that meandered with no purpose or relevance—wasting billions of dollars, years of precious time, and resources that were already limited. Quality and quantity always faltered, and the downstream effects were devastating—confidence lost in an organization, reputations damaged. All because of projects that missed critical marks that actually mattered to a team or organization.

It was only after a lot of hard-earned lessons that the "secret sauce" emerged for building strong, effective projects. A secret sauce that edges teams and organizations beyond the competitive odds, ensures strong organizational reputations, and builds a brand of unparalleled confidence.

It's a secret sauce that can be repeatable, that anyone can use for their own successes, and is outlined in this book.

In essence, this book is for anyone who wants to become well-versed in that secret sauce and

- save time and money,
- identify project needs and goals with greater clarity,
- implement greater efficiencies and productivity, or
- recalibrate a project so that its ROI exceeds expectations.

This book offers guidance and steps for how to establish the above goals—including ones you may never have thought were within your grasp—and then turn them into a reality. If any of these end goals interest you, then the methodology and steps we've created, called **the Relevance Path** or **RELEVANCE**, will inevitably be relevant to you.

THE SEVEN STEPS OF THE RELEVANCE PATH

The Relevance Path and its steps have proven, time and again, to be an invaluable blueprint that helps clients find unforeseen value and success. In the end, RELEVANCE is a means to help our clients employ the correct personnel and technology, identify the right processes, and forge the best strategies for meeting—and often exceeding—their goals and expectations.

RELEVANCE is a methodology that Pathoras created after many years of learning the right way to build projects—and by learning from our many mistakes! It helps teams eliminate all the extra time, money, and effort that's often spent trying to figure out a smart way to move forward with a project.

The Relevance Path is valuable to anyone who works with people, projects, and organizations—even those who find themselves already

THE 7 STEPS TO ACHIEVING **RELEVANCE**

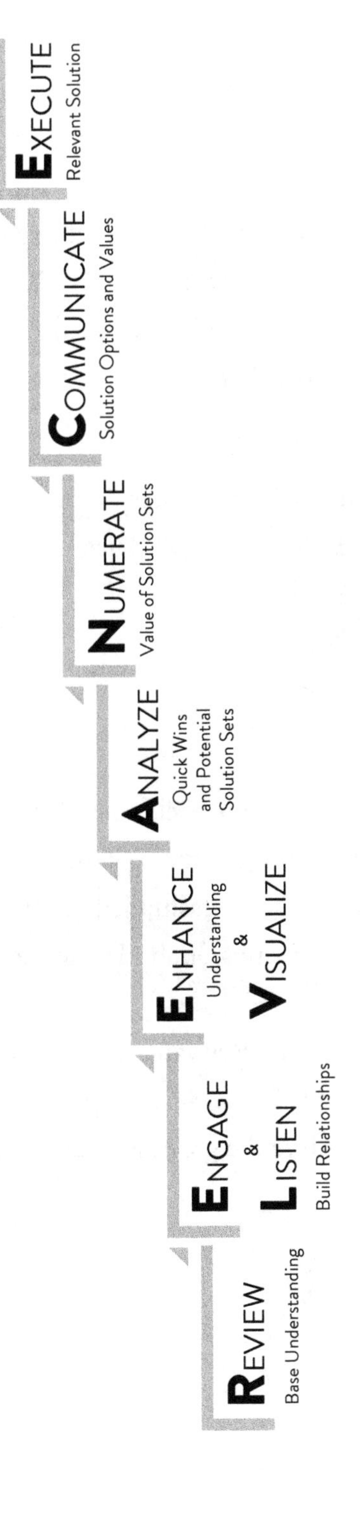

working in a project cycle itself. By using RELEVANCE, projects can save time, money, and resources, and meet goals beyond expectations.

"Relevance" is our secret sauce, the absolute key to our success at Pathoras.

Our RELEVANCE methodology is an acronym for a series of tools that belong to seven RELEVANCE steps to leverage based upon a project's unique attributes. The distinct steps within RELEVANCE each make up a chapter in this book, and they are:

1. **R**eview
2. **E**ngage and **L**isten
3. **E**nhance and **V**isualize
4. **A**nalyze
5. **N**umerate
6. **C**ommunicate
7. **E**xecute

Built within our Relevance Path are a number of other intangibles—empathy, psychology, behavioral economics, and, in some instances, good, old-fashioned common sense—that bind together to deliver both apparent and potentially unrealized successes to our clients.

In short, the Relevance Path provides a vocabulary and toolbox for overcoming barriers that help organizations—as well as our current clients—achieve the greatest results possible.

RELEVANCE:
THE PROACTIVE PROJECT PARTNERSHIP

RELEVANCE was developed by distilling down our many successes into a single repeatable methodology that's comprised of unique and proactive tools.

By using the tools in RELEVANCE, we are able to invest our time more holistically and carefully, while analyzing and vetting our clients' needs, obstacles, goals, and desires. It's a proactive and productive path to a desired destination.

RELEVANCE saves our clients time, resources, and money over the long term thanks in large part to our proactive partnership philosophies:

- Our approach remains focused on helping clients attain their primary—and sometimes unrealized—goals but also applies behavioral economics and psychological applications to ensure smooth-running and clearly communicated projects.
- The Relevance Path allows our clients to achieve their goals in the most efficient way possible.
- It anticipates and addresses the many mishaps that can pop up along the way and finds the quickest and least taxing route, all while carefully identifying the angles and sharp turns where people can get lost or communication can break down.
- RELEVANCE is a framework that can be employed by teams or organizations. It can be used to boost efficiencies and unearth useful processes, as well as aid in workflow management, project management, change management, cyber initiatives, and the overall software development lifecycle.

- It is not, however, meant to replace viable management processes, project management procedures, software development methodologies, or other integral processes. Rather, it addresses efficiency gaps and realigns project outcomes to deliver beneficial results.
- RELEVANCE uncovers real project needs, obstacles, and goals, as opposed to building projects according to perceived needs, obstacles, or goals.
- Therefore, a successful project is one that becomes relevant to a client's particular mission, versus something that the client won't—or will rarely—benefit from. RELEVANCE is, in many ways, a kind of catalyst that helps our clients meet project goals and adds value to their teams and overall organizations.
- RELEVANCE ensures that clients understand the value of project outcomes and the positive implications of attaining those goals. We center everything we do on the concept of RELEVANCE. We filter out distractions and focus on discovering what is relevant to our clients and the project at hand.

The Relevance Path is flexible: It's a carefully crafted set of tools that can be employed at the right time for whatever difficult situations may arise during a project. No two situations are alike, so the Relevance Path can be customized—and adapted—to meet the needs of our clients.

We gauge the success of a project based on how successful the completed project has been in meeting a client's needs. Being and staying relevant is the single most effective way for any person, project, and organization to generate success and find meaningful purpose in their work.

DISCOVERING RELEVANCE BY OVERCOMING NATIONAL SECURITY PROJECT PITFALLS

We founded Pathoras in 2008 because we knew there was a better way to support projects and missions in the national security arena and the intelligence community. It's well known that these are fields where mere seconds can make the difference between life and death.

As time progressed and we embedded ourselves in more complex assignments, we succeeded in missions where others failed. Project after project, we created productivity enablers and established efficiencies for our clients that were relevant to them.

We saved clients millions of dollars. Made their processes more real-time and reliable. Gave our clients valuable time back so they can focus on what matters most to them.

Over time, clients and competitors alike asked us, "How did you succeed here when no one else could?"

These questions forced us to take a step back and come to the realization that we possessed a set of best practices that we were able to employ in all of our collaborations.

It was clear that we needed to formalize these successes, which led to the creation of the refined RELEVANCE methodology you will find in this book. Everything we do at Pathoras travels along this path, which is the reason we can successfully take on so many complex jobs for the intelligence community, national security clients, and corporate customers alike.

We always take the time to get to know our clients and then deliver products, actions, supports, and results that are relevant to our clients' individual needs.

We invest the time needed to discover hidden desires. We recognize and identify true project needs and then deliver them.

Helping our clients achieve extraordinary results is our true calling.

We always strive to achieve results that are better and greater than anything we—or our clients—have ever accomplished before when we work on projects. For us, every project is a journey with that end in mind. So in order to help our clients get to where they want to go, we believe in creating a pathway that will lead them, step by step, toward their definition of success.

We've found that jumping headfirst into a project without proper planning is never a successful strategy. The glide path forward needs to be carefully paved, transitioning from point A to point B. For in the end, establishing trust is the only way to make inroads into uncharted territories.

Think, for example, about a path in the woods or a jungle. The most trusted paths are those that help steer travelers away from poison ivy, quicksand, and other hazards.

We see that as our responsibility. We're guides. Far too often the metaphorical ivy and quicksand that emerges in our industry is the result of ignoring client needs, not paying attention to client objectives, or not communicating the value of a given solution set to a client.

We've used RELEVANCE, while employing one full-time Pathoras team member, to save $2.8 million in nonproductive costs for one client. We've used RELEVANCE to save another client $800,000 when they built a new analytical workflow system. And we've used RELEVANCE to create a 72 percent increase in productivity for one system, closing an audit that was twenty years outstanding.

We've typically seen projects falter in a variety of ways. Some run severely over budget; others fall short in meeting client needs. Some product-based projects prove unsuccessful. And sometimes projects falter because there isn't enough attention being paid to the political dynamics underlying the project.

Sometimes not enough time is taken to truly understand everybody who's involved with the process, which results in failing to achieve the project's true objectives. There are also instances when clients themselves have absolutely no trust or confidence in the support they're receiving.

Often productivity losses and budget overruns are the result of clients who are not in step with a project team, or conversely, a project team is not in step with the client. Sometimes no one is on the same page until the Relevance Path ensures they find a way to get on same page.

The Relevance Path was created specifically to prevent those typical project missteps from occurring. When it comes to national security, there is little to no margin for error.

Because of this, clients have hired Pathoras at the beginning of a project as well as when they believe greater results can be achieved on a project that has already begun. (It is not unusual, for example, for us to be called in when their current support team has run into trouble.)

In the end, we've created a methodology that is extremely flexible and extremely efficient. It's been built to aid all kinds of clients who are facing all kinds of issues. It helps steer you clear of the many project pitfalls we've experienced along the way. It maximizes your chances for success and allows you to find efficiencies and achieve mission goals that you might not have even thought possible at the start of your project. And, most importantly, it also helps your return on investment (ROI) soar.

So join us as we take you on a guided tour of the extraordinary places that the Relevance Path can take you and your organization.

CHAPTER ONE

The Relevance Path™: Setting and Staying on the Right Course with the Right People

Do not go where the path may lead. Go instead where there is no path and leave a trail.

—Ralph Waldo Emerson

MAIN POINTS:

- Like most successful businesses, Pathoras's **project teams** are comprised of resilient, empathetic, and multitalented individuals. But talent and diversity alone don't always equate with success. At Pathoras, our team exudes the skills to maximize a project's RELEVANCE and prevent it from veering off course.
- RELEVANCE has been designed to help clients discover and utilize processes that achieve productivity and efficiencies that far exceed what they ever imagined.

A STORY OF SAVING LIVES AND WORKING SMARTER WITH THE RIGHT PEOPLE AND RELEVANCE

During the early days of Pathoras in fall 2008, our staff of industry veterans was facing a big challenge. Our team supported a project where intelligence analysts sifted through large swaths of data on a daily basis. Their task was simple: to identify important operational leads that needed to be sent to other intelligence officials for further study. Their task was critically important, as these operational leads could wind up saving lives.

But the ability to save lives was nearly impossible with all the problems this project was experiencing. First, there was an exhausting amount of data for analysts to examine. Day in and day out, more data piled up, creating an ever-growing backlog of documents that hadn't yet been looked at but needed to be processed.

Second, our client believed the best way to eliminate this crush of excess data was simply to bring in more analysts to examine the documents—an aim we quickly identified as our client's ***success threshold*** and a contributing factor to the growing ***relevance gap*** (facets of the Relevance Path that we'll discuss in chapter 2).

This project, like all projects, had the potential to excel. And RELEVANCE could help it. So we employed our own intelligence and data analytics to develop a better approach. We leveraged personnel within Pathoras who had previously served as analysts and began exploring different ways to help our client's analysts work smarter, not harder. It soon became evident that our client's approach wouldn't efficiently meet their true needs. Bringing in additional analysts would not only stunt daily productivity but also lead to skyrocketing project costs.

Here's why. Over the course of a single workday, analysts would tire as they processed documents, which meant analysts typically identified fewer and fewer leads as the day progressed. This resulted in stunted productivity and prevented clients from processing all critical documents.

Andy, the cofounder of Pathoras and a master of employing simple but smart solutions, took the time to better understand our client's analytic workflow. He listened to the client and reviewed the situation. From Andy's perspective, it was clear that leveraging a technical solution to automate lead identification could cut through all the "white noise" data. With this, he realized, the backlog could be eliminated altogether.

But what good is a solution if its value is not understood by those who need it? We needed to enlist the right people to help our client realize the value of automation, which could eliminate duplicative records and reduce the time spent reviewing those duplicate documents. This could greatly boost productivity, since documents would still be reviewed (just not their duplicates). Yet as far as our client was concerned, "automation" was a four-letter word, all because the *value* of automation was not clear to the client.

The analyst team didn't understand the value either. By choosing to automate, analysts believed they'd lose their jobs and companies would lose valuable billable hours, a pervasive fear in that office. By introducing automation in a palatable way, however, Andy realized he could save our client money, manpower, and resources, while eliminating its data backlog. In addition, our services would help improve accuracy and help analysts—especially new analysts—better identify important information at the end of their workday. Analysts could improve effectiveness, a clear value.

After discussing these possible solutions and the value they'd bring, our client agreed to employ automated shell scripts that we created, which was a way to use software scripting to achieve an organized workflow.

By employing the right personnel with the ability to translate, communicate, and execute our client's needs into real successes, we were able to achieve the following results:

- Our client's supposedly "insurmountable" backlog was eliminated.
- Analysts' jobs were preserved (much to their pleasant surprise).
- Analysts no longer failed quality-control reviews and enabled a near 98 percent accuracy on all quality-control reviews.
- All duplicates were eliminated.
- Analysts became able to quickly sift through important information, resulting in writing more robust, higher-quality reports.
- Analysts had more time to do what mattered most.
- Nonproductive costs dropped.
- Office morale skyrocketed.

Everyone benefited.

This experience has helped all of us at Pathoras understand why it's so important to communicate value in everything we do, whether it's for friends, family, coworkers, or, of course, clients.

> **RELEVANCE IS A PATH TO SUCCESSFUL OUTCOMES BEYOND EXPECTATIONS.**

It has also helped to shape the foundation of the Relevance Path because RELEVANCE is our proven means of identifying value and saving time, money, and resources on any project. RELEVANCE is a path to successful outcomes beyond expectations. It is a way of life at Pathoras, a collaborative journey and proactive partnership with our clients that is reflective of our experience with creating a win-win situation for our client, the analysts, and the mission alike.

PATHORAS:
CREATING PROJECT CATALYSTS AND HEALERS

People often ask, "What is Pathoras?" Think of it this way: We are a group of chameleons, a multifaceted team of personnel that meld office and business missions with efficient processes, people, technologies, and communication strategies. We save our clients time, money, and resources by helping them to attain the real goals that they wish to achieve.

Our team's multifaceted makeup has allowed us to generate successes for our clients in ways other companies simply can't replicate. For this reason, we've been called "Project Catalysts" and "Project Healers" for those unfortunate projects that need positive momentum or are in distress.

Each one of us possesses multiple skills sets. For example:

> Scott Miller, our COO, has a finance background but has also served as a database developer and a mission analyst. Scott has singlehandedly produced efficiencies for companies in revealing financial data that had downstream effects on consumers.
>
> John Patrick has a background in all-source analytics but also is a scripter and technical information management officer. John Patrick successfully translates mission needs into technical execution, and John Patrick has been cited as "having a measurable impact on mission ... and as such, [information] is going up to the White House" regarding his support to managing data sets.

> Sarah Hewitt, one of our team managers, has a background as a project manager, business process engineer, and mission analyst. Sarah's been known as the "glue" holding offices together and was key in the consolidation of twenty legacy systems into an enterprise system which addressed a major challenge in the organization's strategic direction to manage resources in times of fiscal austerity.

It's our people that allowed us at Pathoras to formalize our success into the Relevance Path.

The second question others typically ask is the following: "What compelled you to start Pathoras?" Our response is always the same, and it is part of that secret sauce to catapulting projects forward for success. Our answer is borrowed from a mantra that Andy—my husband and the chief strategy officer at Pathoras—has always lived by: *work smarter, not harder* to support mission-critical needs.

Working smarter is essentially serving as the catalytic "chemical reaction" to better end results. It also helps redirect projects in need of some care and feeding. In many ways, "working smarter" can be achieved by implementing smarter processes and efficiencies. In others, it's enacting the right communication protocols. By doing so, our nation's security can best be supported and we can better protect America.

Identifying and generating efficiencies often takes a fresh set of eyes. This is where the project healing comes in. Our clients' projects are too vital for time, effort, and resources to be wasted. Implementing RELEVANCE-related efficiencies—even when a project is in distress—works for a large swath of clients, including those who

- are disenchanted with current office processes, abilities, or technology.

- are looking for a better way to conduct daily processes and meet project objectives.
- want to stretch their wings to reach new levels of abilities within a team, organization, or office.

At Pathoras, we specialize in helping our clients weed out any white noise and prevent them from straying onto nonproductive paths. This enables our clients to spend their precious time pursuing aims that truly matter.

Enabling clients, teams, or organizations to focus on what truly matters all starts with the right personnel to execute the right practices and to launch stalled or strayed projects forward.

Time and again, our methodology exceeded client expectations and healed projects. In one instance, our Relevance Path helped a client cut turnaround response times on requests from two weeks to two hours, a 16,000 percent increase in process productivity (further explained in chapter 5).

We've served as the catalyst on other projects. We worked with another client who had spent upwards of $1 billion over ten years on an IT project and still didn't see a positive result. We arrived with our RELEVANCE methodology in hand, and within six months, we were able to successfully implement an information-sharing portal prototype that served as a best practice for the entire industry. We believe we can achieve similarly exciting results for every potential client who reads this book.

COMMON PROJECT MISTAKES AND HOW TO OVERCOME THEM

We once worked in the same office that handled a project where the client was adamant that a simple, clean, commercial-off-the shelf

(COTS) solution would solve all their problems. The team supporting the project didn't have the right backgrounds to clearly communicate that the client's needs would not be supported by that COTS solution. Sadly, the team didn't care either, as they were rotating out of the office in the next few months. What resulted was a costly $900,000 software system that was shelved, never to see the light of day in that office again.

Our experience witnessing the above COTS implementation is indicative of so many other projects and their costly mistakes. Projects that we've been brought in to save were doomed from the start because the path they started down was flawed or the people they had lacked the key skills or drive to connect with the clients.

It's those mishaps that have allowed us to establish RELEVANCE project teams, constructed from best practices to overcome six areas where teams, organizations, or businesses make mistakes in identifying people to build successful projects.

COMMUNICATE EFFECTIVELY (WITH CLIENTS AND STAKEHOLDERS)

So many traditional project teams consist of people who lack the ability to communicate effectively with their clients. A project is only valuable if the workflow, data, and benefit within it can be accurately and clearly communicated to a client.

At Pathoras we've proven, time and again, to be successful in bridging the communication gap between the known and the unknown, in acting as a translator for the language barrier between subject matter experts and end users. It's imperative to employ thoughtful personnel who can clearly communicate best practices for identifying project objectives and measure project progress through clear, concise communication practices such as those identified in RELEVANCE (more on this in chapter 7).

MULTIFACETED SKILLS TO SEE BIG-PICTURE NEEDS

Many projects employ "experts" who excel in a specific discipline but are stove-piped in their ability to bridge disciplines for providing bigger picture benefits.

It's critical to involve people who speak "two languages"—that is, team members who can speak to client needs and mission understanding as well as business processes, workflow management, project management, change management, cyber initiatives, or the software development life cycle. Ultimately it's our multifaceted and multiskilled team members at Pathoras who make the biggest difference by constantly building bridges between clients and their objectives or between clients and their contracted resources.

IDENTIFY REAL CLIENT NEEDS AND GOALS

First and foremost, some project teams don't invest the time necessary to understand their clients, a project's history, or potential pitfalls that may emerge in the future. They also often lack the training needed to extrapolate a client's real goals and a project's real needs. Projects become riddled with ineffective or irrelevant requirements, and the project itself loses purpose.

It's essential to identify people who have the ability to relay the value of solutions to clients in a way that will resonate, including communicating in easy-to-digest layman's terms when needed. This often necessitates the need for multifaceted personnel who can discern client and user needs while being able to identify and communicate big-picture solutions to satisfy those needs (more to come on this in chapter 6). In order to identify project inherent needs, it's also often essential to embed multifaceted, multiskilled personnel with clients to generate the best results (more to come on this in chapter 4.).

RELEVANCE, for example, has taught us that systems analysis and design development are less about technologies and more about the art of communicating needs, obstacles, and goals with people. When IT issues are handled well, they are looked at in response to clients' needs. This is all based upon people that can understand office dynamics and identify positive attributes to expand upon, as well as areas that can benefit from improvement.

ENERGIZED BY EXPANDING CLIENT ABILITIES

So many projects are supported by personnel that are merely collecting a paycheck, without the drive or desire that comes with innately understanding the (positive or negative) impact they can have on a client.

It's important to employ personnel who have a sense of purpose in enabling their client's missions versus personnel whose eyes glaze over at the prospect of working toward a client's goals (versus their own personal goals; more to come on this in chapter 2). RELEVANCE has allowed us to take an entirely different approach to employing talent at the source. Because the seven steps in RELEVANCE take drive and dedication, employing the Relevance Path throughout our processes has allowed us to attract personnel who think like us. Personnel who see challenges as opportunities to excel. Personnel who enjoy thinking outside the box and are thrilled by the challenge of expanding a client's abilities.

VESTED IN PROJECT SUCCESS

Projects often falter because the people taking them on aren't vested in them, or don't see the value in the project itself. This often happens when a project team doesn't agree with the project objectives put forth by the client. Dissension among the team occurs, and those supporting the project lack or lose the motivation needed to propel the project forward.

It's imperative that the personnel supporting a project understand the client's vision and learn the purpose behind the client's project. Doing so invokes motivation. The Relevance Path demands that personnel assume a vested interest in understanding the nuances of complex situations and remain passionate about generating efficiencies that support missions rather than just checking a "Project Complete" box (more to come on this in chapter 8).

ENJOYMENT IN BUILDING CLIENT RAPPORT AND EARNING CLIENT TRUST

Projects often have personnel that shy away from client interaction for one reason or another—fear of overwhelming the client, concern for bothering the client, or anxiety over communicating with the client. In all these scenarios (among many others), a chasm is created where the client is left wondering what the project statuses and updates are. Mistrust and a lack of rapport are bred throughout the team.

It's essential to establish a project culture (as well as the processes that support it) that encourages client interaction. Building a culture of engagement and listening to a client is critical for establishing such rapport, which includes processes RELEVANCE employs to boost project confidence (more to come in chapter 3).

To overcome such pitfalls, project teams are best custom built for each project, based upon the six areas for success above. Teams can be comprised of a project manager, RELEVANCE specialist (in requirements form), business process specialist, workflow manager, and IT specialist, to name just a few.

Given their experience, merely one or two Pathorians can take on multiple roles within a project. We've deployed RELEVANCE in national security projects to successfully pinpoint mission needs. One time, for example, we had one Pathorian serve as the intermediary between technical and analytical teams to create an information-sharing portal designed for communication between two defense agencies. This passionate Pathorian served as a business process specialist, mission analyst, workflow manager, and requirements/RELEVANCE specialist. The portal was hailed as a best practice for the entire defense community—and saved millions in nonproductive costs.

When employing the right personnel, every project that uses the Relevance Path can see great gains. Our project teams build a Relevance Path, and our clients have to be comfortable enough with that path—as well as our team members—in order to traverse it.

By using our Relevance Path methodology, we can fully engage and listen to our clients early in our partnership and determine the best people to support their success.

CHAPTER 1 KEY TAKEAWAYS

By employing similar approaches to those in the case study of "A Story of Saving Lives and Working Smarter with the Right People and RELEVANCE" with the aid of our specialized RELEVANCE methodology, we have been able to show, without question, that such successes can be reproduced time and again with any client that requires our services or employs the right people to meet known and unforeseen project goals.

Pathoras's **project teams** comprised of resilient, empathetic, multiskilled talent that understand how projects stray from purpose—and how to maximize project RELEVANCE—is critical to project success.

CHAPTER

TWO

The Review Step: The Basis for Maximizing ROI

Do not be afraid to walk the path that you must go just because you cannot see the end. The path becomes clearer as you continue to go on.

—Tracy Allen

MAIN POINTS:

- The Review step conducts a fresh end to end review of the project, expected outcomes, key milestones, as well as the relevance gap and success threshold. This step is the basis for additional follow-on reviews throughout the project to determine if the project path is still on the right path or if a path adjustment is required, based upon variables and circumstances that arise.
- The **relevance gap** occurs in every conceivable project and is a knowledge/communication chasm between what an organization perceives the project goals to be and the project team's ability to convey the benefit of the most beneficial project solution(s). To maximize project ROI, it's essential that a project team (1) revisits a project's relevance gap and (2) communicates an effective approach

forward to ensure people, projects, and organizations are and remain relevant and goals are made a reality.

- Defining and revisiting the **success threshold** throughout a project not only measures the impact of actions taken but also ensures they benefit a project. (Otherwise, they're not worth doing.)

In any project we work on (whether it's a system design, a business process workflow, or a variety of other project types), we always start with the **Review step** of our Relevance Path methodology.

The Review step is as transparent as it sounds. Whenever we use the tools from this step, we thoroughly review (and revisit) what we know about the project up to that point while looking ahead to see if there's a gap between project goals and unforeseen project potential.

Why? Because this much is indisputable: You'll never get where you want to go if you don't know where to begin and what guideposts to follow at the onset of your journey to get you to that amazing end destination. The Review step of RELEVANCE is focused on exploring the early steps we take in our collaborative processes—as well as tools that are revisited throughout the time on a project—to ensure project goals are relevant at all times. The tools in this step, such as the *relevance gap* and *success threshold,* as well as the right mix of talented project team personnel, are unique tools that only Pathoras and the Relevance Path uses. They allow our clients to experience a greater return on their investments than they ever thought possible.

In the previously mentioned case, "A Story of Saving Lives and Working Smarter with RELEVANCE," in chapter 1, we reviewed the current state's obstacles and goals and compared them to solutions that could overcome the obstacles and exceed the perceived goals. In the end, we were able to determine that the project—and our clients' analysts—could obtain better reports and produce more of them if they looked beyond simply adding additional manpower.

Like the above example, the Review step gives us the tools required to identify our initial understanding of our clients' objectives and ascertain whether those objectives accurately align with what our clients actually need. All too often our clients' undiscovered—but real—goals can't be achieved by the plans that are currently in place. Instead, those plans reach unnecessary, costly, and inefficient perceived goals.

Two concepts that are critical to generating success (and preventing unnecessary, costly, and inefficient activities) stem from what we call the **relevance gap** and the **success threshold.** Both phenomena are tools that we alone at Pathoras have identified and developed.

They're so important that they represent the foundation of the Relevance Path's review step and can ensure the successful completion of any project. In other words, these tools provide context for our client's core requirements. These practices allow us to better understand our client's true needs and goals.

THE RELEVANCE GAP:
TWO SHIPS PASSING IN THE NIGHT

RELEVANCE is about finding and preserving project meaning. In November 2018, Harvard Business Review published their *Meaning and Purpose at Work* report, which, among many other significant statistics, revealed that more than 90 percent of survey respondents were willing to trade a portion of lifetime earnings for meaningful work. And meaningfulness translates to RELEVANCE.

RELEVANCE IS ABOUT FINDING AND PRESERVING PROJECT MEANING.

Many Americans don't feel that their work is relevant or that the processes, workflows, and business or office missions they support are worthwhile as well. This, itself, is a cultural problem. With meaningless activities come a lack of purpose and a lack of productivity. So feelings of irrelevancy and idleness skyrocket for people, processes, and projects overall. Not understanding purpose results in flawed goals. Value is lost and the right path forward becomes clouded. All of this translates to a critical phenomenon we've identified as the **relevance gap**.

The relevance gap is a time-related phenomenon that presents itself as the gap—sometimes it's a chasm—between what a project team (typically comprised of "subject matter experts" building a solution) knows about the value of a project solution and what clients believe is possible in a project, or understand as the value of a solution. Rarely do we see a project team take the time to discover project potential through activities such this review step of RELEVANCE, let alone communicate that potential to the client. Therefore, the relevance gap occurs in almost every project, and is the difference between what a project team and client understand about a project and its true potential. It's like two ships passing in a night. They never see each other and fail to realize how they could've worked together for the betterment of both crews. The relevance gap typically increases, and the goal is to eliminate the relevance gap so the client understands project potential just like the project team does (more to come on this). The relevance gap is a positively correlated phenomenon; as time increases, so does the relevance gap.

RELEVANCE GAP OF SUBJECT MATTER KNOWLEDGE: INABILITY TO UNDERSTAND RELEVANT SOLUTIONS **WASTES** TIME, MONEY, RESOURCES; **RESTRICTS** RELEVANT, SUCCESSFUL, VALUED OUTCOMES

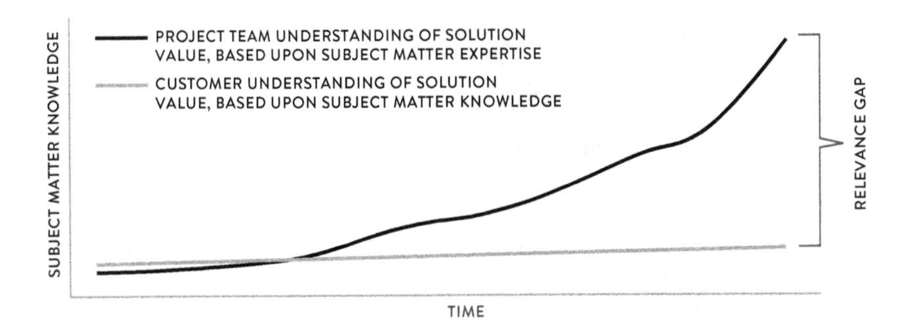

Here's why you may experience a growing relevance gap as time goes on:

- You may lack the time, background, or resources necessary to understand cutting-edge technologies or process and workflow efficiencies that serve as productivity enablers in a given project.
- A project team deepens its understanding of what you need to find success, but that understanding and value isn't conveyed to you.
- The most efficient solutions for your desired objectives aren't identified for you by your project team as technologies evolve or the subject matter becomes more complex.
- You may be unaware that your laborious processes and projects can be improved, since the project team supporting you doesn't see it as their responsibility to discover all the possible solutions and innovations for a project.
- Project teams supporting you pursue the "new" instead of the "necessary," devoting unnecessary time to so-called "cool" features that never wind up delivering you any quantifiable, impressive bottom-line results.

- Project teams supporting you begin without really understanding the right outcomes.

The relevance gap occurs in every conceivable project you can think of, and the ideal relevance gap is one that is eliminated completely.

For example, in one office we supported, a team of computer forensics officers needed to turn around reports on their findings quickly. Yet the tools they used to compile their findings were antiquated, since the software development team supporting them had taken years to develop tools that were not useful to the officers' needs. Our team knew that a series of simple software scripts and tweaks of a few existing processes could compile information in near-real time.

Talking about process or workflow—and current efficiencies or lack thereof—right from the start is critical in reviewing a project's needs. In not doing so, clients fall beyond their maximum capable productivity and a big, fat relevance gap rears its ugly head. The two ships once again pass each other in the night, going in completely separate directions reminiscent of the separating lines on the relevance gap graph above.

ELIMINATING THE RELEVANCE GAP:
A FLEET UNITED

Now that we've discussed how the relevance gap occurs, how do we overcome it?

As we previously mentioned, oftentimes our clients don't have the time or the subject matter knowledge to execute needed objectives based upon their current knowledge, skills, or abilities.

This is the primary reason why clients employ our project teams. Our teams identify the depth of this relevance gap and work with our clients to eliminate it.

When our project team understands the real needs and goals of our clients—that is, who are the right resources and people to enlist to ensure we reach the success threshold—we can eliminate the relevance gap altogether.

SUCCESSFUL, VALUED, RELEVANT OUTCOMES DESTINED BY EMPLOYED RELEVANCE PHASES: QUALITY, PRODUCTIVITY, EFFICIENCY, AND EFFECTIVENESS **ENABLED**; MONEY, TIME, AND RESOURCES **OPTIMIZED**

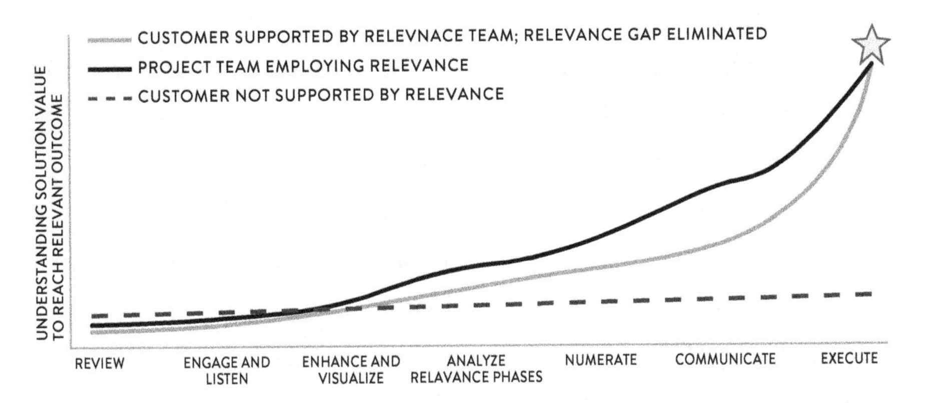

Here's how you can eliminate a growing relevance gap as time goes on:

- Employ a project team that deepens your understanding of what you need to find success and conveys that understanding (and the true value of proposed solutions) to you.
- Leverage project teams that can help you understand or identify the most efficient solutions for your desired objectives, even as technologies evolve or the subject matter becomes more complex.
- Utilize project teams that focus on "necessary" versus "novel" or "faddish" project features; this prevents your time and money from being wasted. Project teams at Pathoras aim to ensure you don't devote unnecessary time to so-called "cool" features that never wind up delivering any quantifiable, impressive bottom-line results.

At Pathoras, we ensure our project teams do all of the above to deliver you success and eliminate the relevance gap. We work to ensure that projects are never begun without really understanding the right outcomes and that our collective time is spent identifying the real needs and goals.

Eliminating such a gap ensures our clients understand the best and most efficient path forward as well as the value of not straying from that path.

What's vital in RELEVANCE—as well as client satisfaction in general—is our ability to help our clients understand the value of optimal solutions (more to come on this in chapters 5, 6, and 7).

It's our responsibility to establish trust and help clients understand a given set of requirements as well as communicate the quantified value of using subject matter knowledge. As a result, our project teams thoroughly eliminate any relevance gaps.

Effective communication is critical to a project's success no matter how ideal a solution or other advance might be. If it is not explained to clients in a way that allows them to understand the value of the technological or business process advance, then it loses all value.

The relevance gap must be eliminated, so our clients and project teams move forward on the same path and enable project success.

Eliminating the relevance gap affords us the opportunity to be on the same page with our clients (reminiscent of the two lines approaching the star in the relevance gap graphic on the previous page). If we all understand the value of our actions—and our path going forward—we can be a fleet of ships united in our journey. We'll reach an agreed upon destination that benefits everyone, regardless as to whether it's under the veil of darkness or the glow of sunlight.

CASE STUDY:

PLUG IN THE PROJECT VALUE TO ELIMINATE THE RELEVANCE GAP

Let me give you an example. At Pathoras, we've worked with one client for nearly ten years now. In the beginning, our client's solutions mirrored our own. But as technology advanced, we realized we could implement plug-ins, which are software features that create customized efficiency for a system, for different client systems that would eliminate unnecessary efforts. Our client didn't understand what a plug-in was, let alone the fact that it could be a solution for efficiency. As a result, a relevance gap formed.

We had to explain and demonstrate the value, in simple terms, as to how it would reduce redundancies and provide auditing functionality, two items our client didn't realize were possible but desperately required in order to strengthen their system security. Only then could we eliminate their relevance gap and open our client's eyes to the great value our solution would provide to their missions and processes.

REVIEW PHASE:

QUESTIONS TO REVIEW TO ELIMINATE A PROJECT'S RELEVANCE GAP

It's our duty at Pathoras to identify and explain a solution's value, a responsibility we take very seriously. One of the most valuable competitive advantages our project teams bring to the table is our focus on continually maintaining and building subject matter knowledge for the betterment of our clients and eliminating the relevance gap.

At Pathoras, we are focused on ensuring that projects remain relevant—that they have worth and permanence—by taking the time to identify relevance gaps and eliminating them.

We will often ask some the following questions during internal project reviews during this Review step to help identify whether there's any relevance gap lurking in the shadows.

Here's how we used those questions to solve the plug-in mystery for our client:

INTERNAL QUESTION ASKED	ANSWERS TO HELP IDENTIFY POTENTIAL RELEVANCE GAPS
What does our client perceive their project to be?	A more robust security system for their computer program that would prevent insider threats.
Are a client's perceived needs the same as what our project team believes is actually needed to reach the correct end goal?	No. The client initially thought a security update in the form of a patch was all that was needed to maintain strong security protocols.
Are there specific resources that our clients are aware (or unaware) of that are needed to meet these goals?	Yes. Our client was unaware that a plug-in could help create better 360-degree security protection.
Are those resources the right resources to meet our client's end goals?	No. Security patches aren't the only resources needed to prevent insider threat. For example, auditing functionality in a system can assist.
What are our client's beliefs regarding actions, processes, tools and efficiencies in meeting those objectives?	Belief that the current actions are sufficient (but potentially lacking), until new security protocols are available or new insider threat directives are issued by leadership. This would be a strong reason to bolster security activities in support of those new directives.
Is our client open to identifying solutions that go beyond their perceived needs toward more optimal outcomes?	Open to ideas but hesitant to employ, being initially unaware of the value of new ideas.

In many instances, it's not a client's responsibility to continuously learn a particular subject matter while managing a project. The time commitment to do so is completely inefficient and unproductive.

Take the plug-in example above. Without a technical background, the ramp-up time for our client to examine what exactly a plug-in is, how it's used, and what plug-in to employ would be completely inefficient.

Our client possesses expertise in other areas, so it's best to allow us to provide such solutions and do the heavy lifting here so that our clients can focus on what really matters to them and what they excel at.

THE SUCCESS THRESHOLD:
A JOURNEY TO COSTCO

In its simplest form, the **success threshold** is our client's desired goal or destination. It's where our clients need to go to sufficiently achieve their goals. The majority of the time our clients exceed their goals (and the success threshold) and reach newfound potential because they employ RELEVANCE. With RELEVANCE, the focus always comes back to our clients' needs and thus enables our team to exceed base expectations and set a new and higher success threshold.

Let's use an example to demonstrate the success threshold.

Think, for a moment, about shopping at a big-box warehouse store. In my house, we're big fans of Costco, which offers value by selling products at wholesale prices. Who doesn't love that? But as we have come to know all too well, spending resources on things we don't actually need can be wasteful as well.

I once bought a case of chicken stock from Costco so I could make my husband, who was feeling under the weather, some chicken soup, which is our family's version of penicillin.

At the time, I convinced myself we needed an entire case of stock. I said to myself, "What if we need to make another batch? What if I need more stock for different recipes?" I assumed I simply couldn't live without that big case of stock, so I bought a crate full of the stuff at Costco.

As it turned out, I only used two cans and the other twenty-two ended up expiring. That momentary sense of urgency that I experienced at that store felt like it was a real and viable need. In truth, I could have gone to my local grocery store, bought two cans of stock (my true success threshold), and I still would have been able to make our soup, while saving money in the process. The cost of making my homemade soup rose ridiculously because I didn't align my perceived needs with my actual needs.

At Pathoras, we've seen examples of this kind of thinking in far too many projects over the years, both in the public and private sectors.

Projects get weighted down by a false sense of urgency and improper planning, which forces them to go over budget, produce underwhelming results, or yield bruising productivity losses.

Newly developed products and tools get shelved, become dust collectors, or are never purchased in the first place.

Deadlines are rarely met and effective processes don't emerge, resulting in underwhelming performance metrics and an overall poor return on investment.

I once saw a $900,000 software product shelved a month after a client bought it, all because it really didn't meet their needs.

Regardless, all of the above pitfalls are rooted in a fundamental lack of understanding of what the real needs, obstacles, and goals of a particular project truly are.

We have clients call us, totally drained of hope, after years of unproductive activity. These situations can be remedied by using the steps in RELEVANCE, which can effectively reverse course and produce efficient and powerful results.

Examining goals and objectives—our extra step—is a part of what differentiates RELEVANCE from the norm.

Unlike other companies, with the success threshold, we examine whether the "on-paper" goals and objectives are actually what our clients need, so we can make sure twenty-two cans of chicken stock aren't wasted.

REVIEW PHASE:

QUESTIONS TO REVIEW TO IDENTIFY A PROJECT'S SUCCESS THRESHOLD

During the Review step of the Relevance Path, we put on our deerskin caps and play Sherlock Holmes. We investigate what a client's past, present, and intended future situation is as well as where we need to focus our efforts to build true success. We ask a series of questions of ourselves when we review our clients' goals and objectives. These questions ultimately play a pivotal role in prioritizing particular discussions throughout the rest of the project.

For each question below, we'll briefly outline how we used our magnifying glasses to discover the important clues that yielded positive results in chapter 1's "A Story of Saving Lives and Working Smarter with RELEVANCE," about introducing automation to help analysts do their jobs more efficiently and find the leads that ultimately save lives.

SUCCESS THRESHOLD QUESTION	SITUATION
Are there, for instance, potential red flags, key words, and phrases that lead to internal discussions among our project team? Are there red flags that may potentially affect the project outcome?	Adding additional personnel to tackle the volume issues was a red flag.
What are the most basic project objectives?	Develop strategies to accommodate the overwhelming influx of information.
What is our client's timeline? Is that timeline flexible or rigid?	This client had a flexible timeline, but it would've become more rigid if the backlog of information continued to grow.
Did the client craft the objectives? If not, who did?	Yes, the client and its program management team crafted the objectives as to how they wanted to whittle the backlog down.
Is our client's priority time or simply budgetary concerns? Which is the harder line?	The priority was more a question of time, given that our client wanted to add manpower to attack the problem. We recognized, thanks to our script implementation, that we could actually save the client money and increase project quality.

Are there obstacles visible from our ground zero view? Is the project already over budget or is there an overwhelmed workforce unable to successfully meet their daily objectives?	Obstacles included the culture in the office and overcoming the rapid concern that jobs would be axed if automation occurred. The workforce was overwhelmed as well.
Are managers unable to provide insight metrics or identify value propositions to their senior managers to demonstrate and justify project impact?	Managers could identify a growing backlog and could, for the most part, quantify how much it increased on a monthly basis (such quantified increases were unnerving to the client).

Asking questions regarding budgetary matters is not a *faux pas* and can often further reveal project characteristics. Successful budgets, after all, are more complex than simply listing direct costs. On a software development project, for example, we may ask ourselves if our client prefers to spend more resources on an attractive user interface or on system performance.

Identifying a success threshold allows project teams to avoid the kind of wasted efforts that inevitably lead to ineffectual results. Such threshold questions are critical to initiating a successful project start.

By quickly understanding clients' basic logistical needs (time, money, resources, perceived solution to achieve), we can immediately begin establishing a pathway for success while forging strong bonds and connections that will last throughout a project's lifespan.

CHAPTER 2 KEY TAKEAWAYS

At Pathoras we work with teams already employed by our clients as well as end users themselves, whether in the beginning of a project or during it. Much of the time we're enlisted to help because we provide support to all parties in transcending the relevance gap and meeting their success threshold. Again, this is vital for finding success in any project.

It's important to know that the relevance gap may increase and the success threshold may change as new leads or stakeholders emerge. But consistently revisiting the topic of RELEVANCE allows our team to continually eliminate pitfalls and ensure our clients understand the value of the project and solutions going forward.

If there is one macro concept that should be gleaned from this book, it's this: All facets and steps of our Relevance Path—review, engage, listen, enhance, visualize, analyze, numerate, communicate, and execute—contribute to closing the relevance gap. We help our clients find the smoothest and most productive path and then continually guide them by supporting them every step of the way until they find, at the end of the trail, that they've produced the most successful and meaningful outcomes possible.

The review step of RELEVANCE is how we begin establishing the right path. In the next chapter, we'll look at how we extend that path during our engagement step and how we can build upon the path to success started by using the Review step tools of the Relevance Path.

- The **relevance gap** is a phenomenon that presents itself as a gap between what a project team knows about an end-state objective's subject matter and what clients know and/or believe they understand about the subject matter required to meet project goals. The relevance gap is a positively correlated phenomenon: As time goes by, the relevance gap increases as customers lose their inherent ability to understand or identify the most efficient solutions for their desired objectives.

- The **success threshold** is the customer's most basic requirements that translate the minimum goals required to successfully complete a job. Once a team knows the minimum goals, the team can build upon those goals. With RELEVANCE, the focus always comes back to the customer's needs, which enables the team to exceed the customer's base expectations and transcend the success threshold.

CHAPTER

THREE

The Engage and Listen Step: Building Rapport to Boost Organizational Morale and Project Confidence

People you meet on your journey may not always give you direct answers, but listen and observe. Everyone on your path presents a lesson for you.

—Sheila Burke

MAIN POINTS:

- Engaging and truly listening to stakeholders builds relationships based on trust, which boosts project confidence and morale.
- Tools to maximize stakeholder engagement include (but are not limited to) **communications pathmaps**, **engagement dialogues**, and good old-fashioned facilitation.

- Project culture is based upon taking time to engage with all stakeholders and identify their **stakeholder types** and **mentality types**, which reveal each stakeholder's individual project motivations.
- Learning and identifying an organization's dynamics is critical to identifying the appropriate project culture for maximizing project synergies and outcomes.

At Pathoras, we know that gaining our clients' trust is an essential step in forging meaningful partnerships. After all, a project's ultimate success is dependent upon learning from our clients and listening to their needs, perceptions, and goals. Only by listening can we collaborate in meeting client aims and surpassing expectations.

Sometimes when I think about trust, my mind wanders back to my days as a Girl Scout. We took our camping trips and retreats very seriously back then.

The initial days of these adventures were always easy and fun. They were followed by something I was less enthusiastic about: plank-style team-building exercises.

"Cross your hands over your chest, stand on this plank, and fall backward," team builders used to tell us, "and one of your fellow Girl Scouts will be there to catch you." I couldn't help but glare at them. Their assurance that I would somehow fall safely into someone's waiting arms four feet below didn't calm me one bit.

In these moments my mind flooded with questions and my stomach clenched. Did they really care about my best interests as much as I did? Would they really be responsible for making sure I made it safely to the ground? After all, I'd only just met them.

It always took a while, but after I spent time with my fellow troop members and got to know them, my anxiety generally dissolved away.

They were sweet, kind, and thoughtful, the kind of people I knew I could be friends with and trust.

Later, when the time came for me to resume my dreaded position on the plank, I fell backward with little hesitation, knowing that my recently befriended troops had my back.

Although we may no longer have to endure camp-related trust-building exercises, we all still have to rely on others during moments of crisis or fear. Trust, after all, is the foundational building block of all strong relationships.

To achieve everything our clients want to accomplish, they sometimes have to fall backward, confident that we, at Pathoras, will be there to catch them.

I know that it's rare to find that sort of trust instantly. Trust develops over time. It takes dedication and an interest in others, which is why the second step of the Relevance Path—what we call the "Engage and Listen" step—is focused on reassuring our clients that we'll catch them when they find themselves falling backward. It also focuses on boosting organizational morale and project confidence.

To do so requires actively listening to clients and reading between the lines of what they are saying so that we can more precisely understand their personal and professional desires and then translate those values into action.

A UNIQUE PROJECT APPROACH:
THE PROACTIVE LISTENING FACTOR

"Reactive" is an unwelcome term at Pathoras. It's what we consider a traditional project approach, where teams ask their clients what they're looking for and then work to meet those requirements. In developing our Relevance Path, we take a different approach than people often see in the project management space. We focus on intangibles that rarely get discussed in our day and age, things like human interaction, communication, and listening.

Here's another reason why the Relevance Path is different. We ask and listen to what our clients are looking for and why. We learn how they do what they do. We extrapolate the magic—that is, "what could be"—and then identify what they really need, want, and can accomplish with a *proactive partnership,* based on "what could be."

On paper, reactive versus proactive may sound simplistic. But in practice, they can often be the difference between a project that underperforms expectations and one that exceeds them.

Clients often react well to discussions about needs because today's world changes so fast that many of us seem to forget the importance of listening and learning. Processes typically revolve around the idea of "get it done, it'll (hopefully) be good enough, we have so much more to do," regardless as to whether smart, cost-effective actions were taken or not. That's where being proactive comes in. It's about taking the time to fully understand and explore the culture, dynamics, processes, people, and interdependencies that act as the foundation of a successful project—which can only truly happen by listening to clients and their needs and desires.

HEARING THE REAL STORY: LISTENING AND ENGAGING TO BUILD TRUST AND PROJECT SUCCESS

In any successful project, what really matters is actively listening to clients. It's listening that produces results. Active listening within a project setting requires four RELEVANCE factors, all of which help build strong project results. These are (1) identifying project stakeholders, (2) determining stakeholder mentalities, (3) building a communication pathmap (more on this in the communication step, chapter 7), and (4) constructing a tailored project team (as highlighted in the review step, chapter 2).

PROJECT STAKEHOLDERS:

KEY INGREDIENTS IN A DELICIOUS PROJECT SAUCE

It's no secret that stakeholders have a vested interest in the success—or derailment—of a project. (Sadly, we've seen both.) Being inclusive of all stakeholders is critical to understanding the entire project dynamic and ensuring that all stakeholders have their needs addressed.

We define stakeholders as "people, entities or groups that have an impact on the project and its outcome." There are three types of stakeholders: primary, secondary, and tertiary. To better understand each type of stakeholder, think of what it takes to build a thriving vegetable garden, one that yields enough tomatoes to generate a warehouse full of delicious spaghetti sauce.

STAKEHOLDER TYPE	STAKEHOLDERS FOR THE SAUCE	HOW PROJECT BENEFITS
Primary stakeholder: a key player—person, entity, or group—that plays a major role in a project's outcome *(financial, process, resource, supply or ancillary, i.e., people who finance projects, managers, and mission-critical team members)*	Tomato plants, as well as the soil, water, and sun surrounding those plants.	Tomatoes, soil, water, and sun are all needed to successfully grow and produce delicious tomatoes.
Secondary stakeholder: a person, entity, or group whose role in the project outcome directly impacts the project outcome slightly less than primary stakeholders *(managers or team members in offices where the project outcomes are only one factor, and not a major one, in their daily routines)*	Tomato fertilizer and tomato cages.	Tomato cages and fertilizer help the tomatoes grow and absorb enough sunlight to blossom. When paired with our primary stakeholders (sun, water, and soil), they all maximize the quality and quantity of tomatoes.
Tertiary stakeholder: a person, entity or group whose role in the project's outcome only tangentially affects the project's outcome *(downstream users who are infrequently accessed or tangentially benefit from the project outcome)*	Other plants in the garden: basil, oregano, and parsley.	Without basil, oregano, or parsley, sauce can still be made, but not to the level of quality desired. Each bolsters a unique sauce's flavor.

It's also the project team's responsibility to manage, facilitate, and communicate with stakeholders. Not doing so means major project factors could be missed. The sauce may get finished, but it often tastes like a bland concoction of tomato flavor, which satisfies no one.

Identifying and classifying stakeholders is not only an important factor in building engagement but also in achieving positive results. This is why it's so important to classify clients, investors, managers, supervisors, team leads, and end users as stakeholders. In essence, they are any player that has an impact on a project's outcome.

Some project teams consider stakeholders to be nothing more than the clients who financially support the project. We don't. In our minds, such basic thinking becomes a detriment to client satisfaction.

It's important to identify all the project stakeholders because each stakeholder perceives the concept of "value" differently. Some stakeholders may view project value in monetary terms, including how much a process or product will cost or how it will save them money in the long run. This is a value proposition that primary stakeholders often evaluate by looking at the cost-benefit analysis of a given project. Other stakeholders may perceive project success as being able to communicate key concepts efficiently throughout a given team.

Many of our national security clients, by contrast, tend to see great value in being able to effectively produce reports and send them downstream to users in real time or near-real time. On the other hand, many of our clients who crave productivity define value in terms of convenience—that is, the ease and efficiency of using a particular system (more on how stakeholders value projects can be found in the Numerate step, chapter 6).

This is why it's so important to not only classify stakeholders but to understand what the term "value" means to them. Only then can a project team prioritize requirements that best support those aims.

In some cases, it's wrong to assume that stakeholders are going to be completely forthcoming. This may be the result of outside factors we're not privy to, including office dynamics and pending resource allocations or budgetary realignments—or sometimes even a particular professional agenda. In all of these situations, taking the time to establish trust is what creates the best path forward. Making sure to include all stakeholders and their vested interests in the project's outcomes is what will make a mouth-watering, award-winning sauce.

MENTALITY TYPES AND PROJECT CULTURE:
MIND-BOGGLING PROJECT VISION, NO MORE

A **mentality type** is a RELEVANCE- and Pathoras-coined term for what we define as "a culture-based evaluation of how invested clients or stakeholders are in a particular project's outcome and success." Evaluating mentality allows our project team to customize the approaches needed to successfully communicate and work with each client and stakeholder. A strong project culture is needed to produce synergy among stakeholders and it's paramount to creating the right project vision. There are three macro mentality types we have identified which categorize how best to work with those particular stakeholders.

Information seekers are detail-oriented individuals, groups, or entities who want to learn from the RELEVANCE process and will be an active presence throughout the project. They are motivated to become a part of the process, understand the project and its value, and frequently communicate with project leaders. They typically request frequent communication and updates.

Disengaged leaders are people, groups, managers, or entities who often suggest a project outcome is not a high priority on their list. At Pathoras, we don't shy away from working with these leaders. Every disengaged leader is disengaged for a reason, and oftentimes that leader is actually engaged in other efforts that they understand the value of. So it's best to take the time to learn what a client's priorities are and work accordingly. We still provide the best product possible, and many times our projects have enabled disengaged clients to succeed on other projects or goals. Many of our clients have even won awards because of those projects we supported (that they were initially disengaged with).

Middle-of-the-Road Players (MOTR, pronounced "motor") are persons, groups, or entities who typically know little about the project or its trajectory and benefit from learning more about a project's limitations and capabilities.

No matter what type of mentality a client or stakeholder has for a project, it's best to work with them all, tailoring communication so that it resonates with the client and stakeholders for a unified project path forward.

Striving to be open to reevaluating stakeholder status and mentality types as projects progress is also important for many reasons. First, stakeholder status is dependent upon project goals. For example, should a linguistic shop suddenly require translation standards for Somali language interpretations, a Somali linguist may quickly become a primary stakeholder.

Second, whenever a client or stakeholder turnover occurs, it often leads to a gap in knowledge. We've found that it's critical for any project team to revisit this case with a new client and then establish a relationship with the new client or stakeholder so everyone can move forward together on the same path.

CASE STUDY:

IDENTIFYING STAKEHOLDER AND MENTALITY TYPE: ADDRESSING CULTURE AND OPTIMIZING RESULTS

A series of Pathoras personnel worked for a specific client who dealt with high priority national security missions on a daily basis. The client was always managing multiple tasks, with a variety of downstream customers waiting to receive different types of reports.

When we discussed a way to help streamline all those tasks with the client, we were met with a "deer in the headlights" look. We asked, "Are you interested in learning more if we can help streamline your tasks?" He shrugged half-heartedly. It was clear he was overwhelmed and unaware of any way to make his days easier. He was a primary stakeholder because he oversaw the entire office, so we determined his mentality type was a MOTR player because he was unaware of a trajectory for success to ease his daily burdens.

Since he was a MOTR player, we knew it was critical to provide advice regarding simple solutions that were already available. We saw there was a way to incorporate multiple reports into one salient document that would visually identify critical leads for reports to be sent out. His personnel could more quickly pull together these reports, and it would streamline his ability to review the "bottom line" of each report. The bottom-line direct benefit to him? He could easily approve disseminating reports to the downstream customers. So we said just that, offering advice as to how his days could be easier and his tasks could be completed more rapidly. In this case, it was all about the capabilities we could provide, which yielded no negative limitations.

This provided a logical foundation so we could provide a more detailed follow-up. In the end, the client's deer look transitioned into a grin, and his days were streamlined and more manageable. In addition, the downstream customers were pleased, since all reporting got out to them much more quickly.

At Pathoras, our ability to identify "mentality types" is just as important in generating success as briefing clients is. We have to respect their culture so we can cater the project vision to what best supports their dynamics and overarching objectives. We recognize how important it is to treat each client and stakeholder mentality type in the correct way, which maximizes their desired outcomes and aligns with the project's macro goals.

COMMUNICATION PATHMAP AND ENGAGEMENT DIALOGUE:

CONSISTENT AND CUSTOMIZED COMMUNICATION

It's best to identify stakeholder and mentality types through several activities. Here are two examples: (1) engaging with the client and stakeholders through *engagement dialogues* and (2) explaining how the best path for success will inevitably include a communication plan, a schematic we call our *Communication Pathmap.*

Our **engagement dialogues** are a series of questions our project team asks clients and stakeholders which allow us to tailor our communication plans to each client and stakeholder's communication preferences.

It's here where we begin to assess stakeholder types and mentality types that characterize how we've listened to our client and stakeholders, as well as how we'll engage with them in future communications. A successful example of the engagement dialogue in the Relevance Path is shown below. We've found that our clients or stakeholders don't always have an answer to all of our questions, so we typically come prepared with prototype communication options that clients and stakeholders can pick from:

- What is your role within your organization: investor, manager, supervisor, team lead, end user?
- What's your location?
- What is the preferred mode of communication: in person, email, phone, text, VTC?
- What's your second preferred mode of communication: in person, email, phone, text, VTC?

- How frequently would you like to communicate? Daily, semi-weekly, weekly, biweekly, monthly?
- Is there anything in particular you're interested in receiving updates on more frequently than anything else?
- We've found that projects are most successful when we have the opportunity to sit down with (and shadow) teams so that we can best understand their processes. This is, of course, based upon availability and how long you anticipate it will take for us to learn your processes.
- Would you be willing for us to sit down with you so we can better understand your processes?
- How long do you anticipate our meeting will continue? Hours, days, weeks?
- We also think it's in the project's best interests to sit with your team so we can better understand their processes as well. Are there other personnel in your organization that you recommend we reach out to? It's been our experience that information can and will change throughout a project, based upon given priorities, funding, resources, etc. Based upon your preferred communication mode and frequency, we will communicate those changes and updates to you.

We also make it a point to remind our clients not to hesitate in asking us to change the way we are communicating with them. We then follow up with them to schedule a time where we can better learn their needs and processes as well as ask for further input as the project moves forward.

A **communication pathmap** outlines expectations for status updates, in terms of both frequency and the type of content that will be provided. It helps refine and reveal requirements and the best project goals and is in part based on engagement dialogue questions such as the ones on the previous page.

A communication pathmap and engagement dialogues benefit clients' projects in a variety of ways:

ENGAGEMENT DIALOGUES AND COMMUNICATION PATHMAP BENEFITS	
HOW BENEFITS	***WHY BENEFITS***
Ensures that all stakeholders will receive necessary and relevant status updates	A primary stakeholder who is an investor will likely want status updates on potential timelines and costs, whereas a tertiary stakeholder may only need updates on process changes related directly to his or her daily activities.
Ensures that the right stakeholders are being included in the process	Stakeholders are inherently more invested in a project if they're included in the process.
Establishes expectations for how we will communicate with stakeholders throughout the project	It's critical to respect our client's time while still providing necessary updates. As a result, stakeholders feel comfortable knowing how, when, where, and why they'll get updates.
Enables our project teams to be flexible with our clients' and stakeholders' needs	Opening up the lines of communication offers clients the freedom to change frequency and modes of communication during the project's progression.

Experience has shown that keeping communication pathmaps separate from all other project pathmaps is the key to success. Integrating a communication plan within a project framework tends to breed failure, as communication only gets highlighted at the macro level of a project's framework.

It is essential to maintain a communication pathmap separately so that the importance of clear communication with stakeholders remains respected.

An example of the communication path that we use most frequently at Pathoras includes stakeholder name, organizational role, location, preferred communication frequency, preferred communication mode, stakeholder type, and mentality type.

Our communication pathmap allows us to quickly and concisely compile information that we receive when we're building our framework for our engagement with the client and stakeholders.

Above all, having engagement dialogues with stakeholders and a communication pathmap for the project writ large ensures the project's communication practices are closely aligned with the needs of the project and the mode of communication that best speaks to each stakeholders' needs as well.

CHAPTER 3 KEY TAKEAWAYS

In the end, it all comes down to engagement and listening—truly hearing what the client and stakeholders need. If you take the time to learn about the clients' and stakeholders' interests and preferences, trust inevitably follows. This is critical to surveying the landscape for a possible path forward—and then traversing down that path toward successful outcomes with a united team that trusts the path forward.

- The **communication pathmap** outlines expectations for status updates (frequency, content) and is a critical foundation to build upon.
- **Engagement dialogue** is a series of questions the project team asks customers and stakeholders, where all of the information from the dialogue will be captured in the communication pathmap. The intention of the engagement dialogue is to establish a relationship with customers and stakeholders and to ensure communication plans are tailored to each customer and stakeholder.
- **Stakeholders** are people, entities, or groups who play a role in the project and its outcomes. There are three types of stakeholders: primary, secondary, and tertiary.
- A **primary stakeholder** is a key player (person, entity, or group) in the project's outcome, where the project's outcome is largely impacted by the stakeholder from a financial, process, resource, supply, or influence standpoint.
- A **secondary stakeholder** is a person, entity, or group whose role directly impacts the project's outcome less than that of a primary (key) stakeholder.
- **A tertiary stakeholder** is a person, entity, or group whose role only indirectly or tangentially affects the project's outcome. A

tertiary stakeholder also exists when a project's outcome only has a minor or indirect impact on the person, entity, or group's end goals, finances, resources, or processes.

- **Mentality types** are culture-based evaluations that gauge how vested customers and stakeholders are in the project's outcomes and successes; such evaluations enable the project team to understand the approach and amount of effort needed to successfully communicate and work with each customer and stakeholder. There are three macro mentality types: information seekers, disengaged leaders, and middle of-the-road (motr) players.
- **Information seekers** represent one of three mentality types often present in project customers and stakeholders, defined as detail-oriented individuals, groups, or entities who want to learn from the process and will be an active presence throughout the project.
- **Disengaged leaders** represent one of three mentality types often present in project customers and stakeholders who are people, groups, managers, or entities who are simply checking project boxes; thus the message insinuated to the project team is that the project's outcome is not a high priority on their list.
- **Middle-of-the-road (motr) players** represent one of three mentality types often present who fall into two motr subgroups: those who know little about the project or its trajectory for success and admit as much (*admitters*) or those that know little about the project or its trajectory for success but pretend or insist they know a lot (*deniers*).
- **Admitters** represent a subgroup of the middle-of-the-road player (motr) mentality type who are often present in customers and stakeholders who know little about the project or its trajectory for

success and admit as much; they can benefit greatly from learning more about the project's benefits.

- **Deniers** represent a subgroup of the middle-of-the-road player (motr) mentality type who are often present in customers and stakeholders who know little about the project or its trajectory for success but pretend or insist they know a lot; they can benefit greatly from learning more about the project's benefits.

CHAPTER

FOUR

The Enhance and Visualize Step: Uncovering Real Project Needs, Obstacles, and Goals for Maximum Return on Investment

Many are stubborn in the path they have chosen, few in pursuit of the goal.

—Friedrich Nietzsche

MAIN POINTS:

- Tools such as **embedding** (aka **shadowing**) as well as the **enhancement dialogues** and **refinement dialogues** are critical for project success because they reveal the intent of what is needed, uncovering the real needs, obstacles, or goals for project success.
- Every project has **apparent needs, obstacles, and goals,** as well as latent ones that are just begging to be discovered; it's the project team's responsibility to uncover the **latent needs, obstacles, and**

goals to ensure maximum project ROI (and the *right* project end is achieved).

- Assessing stakeholder responses at a macro level for trends and unique responses in the **E-ToURspectives** assessments and a **Q-ToURspectives** review (discussed in chapter 5) prevents requirements creep and further prioritizes and uncovers hidden (but real) needs, obstacles, and goals.

In every situation, there is always more than what meets the eye. At Pathoras, one of our core values is perseverance, where we always see challenges as opportunities. We see the opportunity to excel for our clients, partners, and the mission.

Though there are many examples, one such situation comes to mind where we were faced with challenges and created success by using tools in the Enhance and Visualize step of RELEVANCE. In this situation, we applied tools such as our enhancement dialogues and shadowing project stakeholders to uncover real project needs on a military ground analytics contract.

We were enlisted to help improve daily workflow processes for a group of military ground reporting analysts (***the apparent need***). Our initial orders were to obtain specific reports requested by analysts and send them those reports. But while shadowing our client's analysts, the Pathoras team conducted an ***enhancement dialogue*** and discovered that a more substantive process change could help analysts write more comprehensive reports (***the latent need***).

Here's why. Analysts were expending valuable time searching more than 600 unorganized folders on a shared drive (***the latent obstacle***). It was a true needle-in-a-haystack scenario. And as a result, analysts rarely found what they were looking for, which meant they couldn't write comprehensive reports that were desperately needed to support and protect the military on the ground overseas.

But our team had experience in analysis, so we recognized the unwieldy labor processes required to write up a report, let alone a complete one (another latent obstacle).

Due to the lack of organized source information, it also became clear that the office desperately needed knowledge retention (another latent need). In hoping to help analysts build upon previously reported subject matter (***latent goal***), a Pathoras analyst with an IT background worked closely with our customer's analysts to enhance production processes.

By identifying potential analytic interests obtained in a set of military data, Pathoras developed automated processes to assist, improve, and enhance the analysts' ability to discover information of interest. Over 65,000 military reports (***a REAL project goal!***), which had been previously strewn across 600 folders, became properly indexed and organized. The net effect was so successful that it was deemed "revolutionary" by the one of the directors of the entire organization.

By discovering latent needs and goals, Pathoras utilized one person to support thirty analysts. Ultimately, our work saved our client over $2.8 million in nonproductive costs in just one year. Such processes more than doubled the productive reporting time of twenty analysts (a 133 percent productivity increase, from 23,400 to 54,600 hours). For the first time, our client was able to meet all of Congress's document requests, gain greater legitimacy within their field, and provide smarter, lifesaving recommendations to the ground troops overseas.

Like the above project, our success was the result of getting to know our client, learning their dynamics, and understanding their motivations. It's no different on a personal level; people don't typically get married after just one date. It takes time to get to know one another and learn each other's desires, habits, quirks, dreams, and goals. This is why our Enhance and Visualize step of the Relevance Path is so critical to project success.

Clients spend precious time and resources working with project teams. It's only logical to feel a responsibility for project teams to internalize a client's desires and goals. This goes for every project, whether it's supported by Pathoras or another team. The keyword here is "enhancement." Using the tools in this step, the central aim is to enhance understanding of every project, including its processes, requirements, and needs.

It's only in cultivating a comprehensive understanding of the issues before us that we can discern the right project needs and identify efficient avenues for success.

This always translates into a large increase in project's ROI for clients and project teams who use the tools in this chapter.

APPARENT VERSUS LATENT NEEDS, OBSTACLES, AND GOALS:

DISCOVERING WHAT REALLY MATTERS

As we touched upon briefly in the above project, a few Pathoras defined terms are critical in ensuring a project's success, to include how we conduct our "Enhance and Visualize" phase: **apparent needs, obstacles, and goals versus latent needs, obstacles and goals**.

Apparent is what appears to be part of a project at the surface level. ***Latent*** is what's uncovered through discussions and shadowing, which is also directly related to a project. Apparent and latent are present in three main ways: needs, obstacles, and goals.

Here is the way we differentiate between "apparent" and "latent" at Pathoras, and we'll use the example of going to the dentist to demonstrate the difference between apparent and latent.

	APPARENT	LATENT
NEEDS	Apparent Need: The requirements that our customers believe are necessary to achieve their stated goals. *Example: A patient may go to a dentist's office thinking that she needs a cavity refilled to ease her pain.*	Latent Need: The hidden requirements that emerge only after we spend time with a customer and unearth the best possible solutions to their given situation. *Example: In fact, the dentist may find that a root canal is actually required to save her tooth.*
OBSTACLES	Apparent Obstacle: Believed to be a known impediment to achieving project goals. *Example: The patient didn't have enough time because of work responsibilities to undergo treatment immediately.*	Latent Obstacle: Hidden impediments to a project reaching its full potential, *Example: The patient then learned the cost of the root canal and worried she would be unable to pay it anyway.*
GOALS	Apparent Goal: Believed and known to be the project objectives. *Example: The dentist worked to find a way to fit the treatment into his patient's busy schedule.*	Latent Goal: Uncovered project objectives that must be accomplished for true project success. *Example: The dentist also had to come up with a payment plan that would make the root canal affordable.*

Identifying apparent and latent needs is a critical first step in enhancing our understanding of the real situation at hand. And as demonstrated above, we must also accept the fact that there may be **apparent obstacles** and **latent obstacles** that are impediments to a project reaching its full potential and meeting critical project goals.

If accepting apparent obstacles wasn't enough, we must also acknowledge latent factors that impact projects. Why? Because when latent obstacles and needs aren't recognized, difficulties inevitably arise, and a phenomenon commonly known as "**requirements creep**" begins to set in. Everyone knows the basic tenets behind requirements creep, even if the actual term may not be familiar to you.

Requirements creep occurs when a project begins to meander off in unexpected and unproductive ways, which in turn leads to wasted time, resources, and money. In other words, it takes more time, money, and resources to properly complete the job.

Not all customers are aware of the many latent needs and obstacles that can emerge in projects, but we are. We know how to find the real project needs, obstacles, and goals to build efficiencies, maximize results, and exceed expectations. But in order to devise the best solutions, we need context. We need to understand everything we can about our clients: their offices, personnel dynamics, processes, and outside environmental factors as well as any variables or potential pressure points in play.

It's never about checking boxes on a to-do list. Too often, traditional project teams will simply say, "We communicated with the customer, and here's what they want." They echo back what their clients tell them, never taking the time to examine the hidden and real issues bubbling beneath the surface. In other words, project teams must take the time to examine the difference between a customer's apparent needs and their latent needs, or for that matter, take into account the apparent obstacles and latent obstacles that can derail a project. Here's why:

> Real = Relevant needs, obstacles, and goals =
> Maximized project success = Increased return on investment

That's the beauty of following our Relevance Path. Clients can come to us with apparent needs, obstacles, and goals; we help them discover their true latent needs and then overcome their latent obstacles. We discern their latent goals, which allows *real* project needs, obstacles, and goals to be completed.

With the tools in this chapter, we eliminate wasted time, resources, and money spent on requirements creep, ultimately increasing return on investment.

MAXIMIZING PROJECT SUCCESS WITH THE ENHANCEMENT DIALOGUES TOOL

Our proactive approach leans on a Pathoras-built project enabler that we call **enhancement dialogues**, which are a series of questions we ask customers to enhance our understanding of the apparent and latent project needs, obstacles, and goals. It builds upon the rapport we've established using tools in the Engage and Listen step. These enhancement dialogues often involve shadowing and interviewing stakeholders by embedding our teams in a client's work environment. By doing so, we can identify a customer's real needs, obstacles, and goals to illuminate the right and relevant path to project success.

Here's a short list of the kinds of enhancement dialogue questions we've found to be successful, as well as why we ask stakeholders each question.

QUESTION:	RATIONALE:
Since our last meeting has anything changed regarding your role in your organization or your preferred mode and frequency of communication?	Because project processes and preferences are fluid, we must constantly refine, update, and clarify our best practices. If stakeholders' preferences change, we update our communication roadmap to ensure we meet their needs.
What are the current processes and tools for communicating information across the organization?	Processes and tools can aid us in identifying stakeholders and courses of action that may have not been considered previously.
Are the processes and tools automated or manual?	We need to target potential areas for process improvement.
What processes appear to be effective in your office?	If processes work, they could be incorporated into potential project solutions.
Which office obstacles could inhibit your organization's success?	Asking this question allows us to identify apparent and latent obstacles that need to be overcome when fixing a project.
Does the proposed project outcome and solution support your business needs and business processes? Why or why not?	This helps us clarify mentality types (Chapter 3) and provides us more context for deciding whether a project outcome is indeed the right solution. It also identifies the stakeholder's perceived project objectives.

Would you be open to considering actions, processes, tools, and/or technology to enable efficiencies and meet project objectives? If so, which actions, processes, tools, and/or technology?	This relates directly to the relevance gap review (Chapter 2) and whether our customers would be open to identifying solutions for greater optimal outcome.
Are there other personnel in your organization you recommend we reach out to?	This query helps us identify potentially unrevealed stakeholders who may also be critical to project success.

We've carefully crafted these enhancement dialogue questions over a number of years for a variety of reasons: to help customers highlight the positive, identify the negative, steer away from flashy and useless data, and refine outcomes and stakeholders—all in order to maximize project success.

First, we want to emphasize the positives before the negatives. Understanding what is working in a given organization always helps us identify the correct solution.

My great friend, mentor, and industry colleague Pete Hatfield, longtime executive with companies such Digital Equipment Corporation, Cray Research, Northrop Grumman, and AECOM, has taught me a host of lessons over the years, including this invaluable pearl of wisdom: When young people are searching for a career, one of the best questions to ask them is what they *don't want* to do instead of what they think want to do. This helps them weed out the white noise and focus on their most viable career path. Over the years, we've found this concept to be equally valuable when dealing with projects and management changes. Identifying what processes are working helps pinpoint viable solutions.

Second, by focusing on the negative, customers often become defensive without even realizing it, which can create problems for customer engagement and implementation. This is why we integrate positive and negative open-ended questions and always ensure we ask questions in a manner that's respectful to our stakeholders. It is not our intention to ask suggestive answers by using yes or no questions. Such questions defeat the purpose of the enhancement dialogue and create a narrative that the project team may *want to see* versus what the true stakeholder narrative *really is.*

Third, we've found that customers usually gravitate toward flashy apparent needs like trendy digital tools as opposed to actual business requirements. We help our clients weed out any of these often unnecessary and expensive approaches so that they can get the best return on their investment.

Fourth, the enhancement dialogue allows us to further refine which stakeholders are critical to a project's outcome while also determining which additional people our team should speak with. This is a critical step in ensuring we're speaking to the right people.

Identifying additional stakeholders can be a lot like a private investigator conducting an investigation. Sometimes the prime suspects are not the people who possess the information required to actually solve the crime. Sometimes stakeholders overlook other stakeholders who are central to the process because they are in a managerial role and simply aren't familiar enough with key subordinate players who have a major impact on a project.

Ultimately, the real beauty of our enhancement dialogues is that they help reveal customer and stakeholder motivations, obstacles, and goals, while achieving maximum project success and relevancy.

THE ART OF VISUALIZATION:
PICTURING YOUR WAY TO IMPORTANT PROJECT INTERDEPENDENCIES

As we complete enhancement dialogues, we use them in tandem with critical visualization tools. As filmmaker and graphic designer Saul Bass is famous to have said, "Design is thinking made visual." An image tends to resonate much better than a block of text, which is why we literally build maps and schematics out of the data we capture. We do this with the client's needs and goals in mind so they can quickly and easily digest the most important information and concepts in one document.

Artists build physical creations based upon inspiration and their impression of the world around them. We build visuals inspired by our client and stakeholders as well as our understanding of their goals and the project (and world) around them.

In this step, one of the most powerful visualization tools we use is a **stakeholder pathmap**. This is a visual chart of stakeholders and stakeholder types (primary, secondary, or tertiary) as well as the relationships between each stakeholder. Stakeholder pathmaps allow our project teams to begin to pinpoint which stakeholders we should revisit while also diagramming any interdependencies and connections between these individuals.

Each of these maps—which look like a network of spider webs on paper—are built out of the responses we receive during our engagement and enhancement dialogues. Over time we've found that using a different shape for each primary, secondary, and tertiary stakeholder makes the diagrams more readable for our customers while also highlighting who is most integral to a given project's success.

We draw connections between stakeholders who have some kind of relationship to each other while also pointing out what kind of relationships they might have (whether they are financial, informational, procedural, or something else entirely). We can now see everyone who will be traveling along the Relevance Path with us as well as why they're integral to the project's ultimate success.

Think of the stakeholder map like an airline route map. Let's use Southwest Airlines as an example. People unfamiliar with Southwest may assume that the airline only has flights servicing the southwestern United States, but by looking at Southwest's route map, it's clear they offer a plethora of direct flights into and out of other areas of the country. The Baltimore-Washington International (BWI) airport, for example, is a hub for Southwest, so Baltimore is a primary stakeholder for Southwest Airlines. Had we not taken the time to really understand Southwest Airline's operations and flight connections, we may have overlooked this important interdependency.

Such key connections and relationships are often revealed because we take the time to develop stakeholder pathmaps. Our stakeholder pathmaps often prove to be invaluable documents because large organizations often neglect to synchronize IT or procedural efforts. For example, this is especially true in the national security arena, a field that is, by its nature, a need-to-know culture that's not prone to sharing information. As a result, similar initiatives often occur simultaneously across different divisions, departments and agencies; the end result is a noticeable lack of interoperability.

Yet our stakeholder pathmaps have identified such parallel processes on numerous occasions, processes each office was unaware the other was partaking in. The pathmaps shed light on this, and in the end, offices collaborated for an end product (and processes) that better complemented both offices.

Our Relevance Path addresses our desire to gain a greater understanding of a client's specific requirements and to obtain broader knowledge regarding what is occurring throughout their organization and their industry in general.

Customers often ask us how we're able to discern, with such accuracy, the independencies within an organization. Such successes often flow directly from our ability to construct accurate stakeholder pathmaps.

CASE STUDY:

MINIMIZING COSTS FOR A FINANCIAL SYSTEM REWORK BY USING THE ENHANCEMENT DIALOGUE AND STAKEHOLDER PATHMAPS TO IDENTIFY REAL GOALS FOR PROJECT SUCCESS

As part of a congressional mandate, a federal client needed to find a way to better manage capital assets in the hope of achieving a clean financial audit (the customer's success threshold and apparent goals). The customer was using a system to house profit data, which was a financial system of record, but it was not connected with a series of other business systems (the apparent obstacle). This meant information was strewn everywhere and not in the financial system used by auditors (latent obstacle). The relevance gap of this project became evident after an initial review of the customer's needs and current situation.

Initially, the client considered reconfiguring his financial system so a complete audit could proceed (the apparent need). One Pathorian, in particular, realized that this would be overly time-consuming and cost-prohibitive (a latent obstacle). This would require large-scale training programs and enterprise-wide communication efforts.

After conducting facets of an enhancement dialogue with the customer and creating a version of a stakeholder pathmap, it was discovered that a key stakeholder had been overlooked: the accountant responsible for the audit information.

For two years the client had erroneously assumed that the procurement officers overseeing the assets were, in fact, the primary stakeholders. But our investigation proved otherwise. We then found that a customized, lightweight application that connected the financial systems to the procurement system would be the best solution to the problem (the latent goal).

Although it took approximately one year and a team of four technical developers to design and build this application, this approach proved to be extraordinarily successful. The application has now been in production for years, and the client's accountants are very pleased with its ability to store all cost-related data in one place so they can perform their accounting magic. Financial auditors can now review capital asset data and are pleased that there is finally enough reviewable data to enable the client to meet its office's congressional mandate.

TOURSPECTIVE REVIEWS:
HOW TO BUILD A TOUR OF THE PROJECT'S BEST DIRECTION

To develop truly relevant goals, we don't stop at identifying a project's primary, secondary, and tertiary stakeholders; we take an additional step to better understand their needs. At this point, we often use a Pathoras-designed tool that we call an **enhancement trends or unique responses** a.k.a. **E-ToURspectives review**. This is a full, top-to-bottom analysis of all the responses we have received from our enhancement dialogues and shadowing sessions. We use this information to identify trends and/or unique responses that merit further review, as well as key takeaways from our findings.

An example of how we use an E-ToURspectives Review can be found at therelevancepath.com.

ToURspectives reviews also allow us to visually (and collectively) see which trends each stakeholder identified as important. Together, the trends and unique perspectives allow us to identify latent goals that weren't previously apparent.

Oftentimes we find that the responses from an individual or a small group of people who have deep knowledge of the project become essential stepping-stones to success. These individuals can be so instrumental in eliminating the relevance gap that their responses deserve to be noted in what we call the "unique responses" part of this review.

Think of our ToURspectives as a tour of the land ahead, allowing us to survey potential obstacles and identify further opportunities for success. We enhance that "tour" with ToURspectives visuals: image-rich documents that include impressive statistics, results, and trends gleaned from the ToURspectives review.

Identifying trends and/or unique responses is so important that we use various forms of a ToURspectives review throughout other RELEVANCE steps, too (including a Q-ToURspectives Review in chapter 5, and Gallery Walk ToURspectives Review and User Session ToURspectives Reviews in chapter 8).

Everyone's time is valuable and limited. So the ToURspectives reviews are designed to help our primary stakeholders and users grasp results quickly and comprehensively so that we can get the best responses possible. This critical in discovering the best potential paths ahead and why those paths are worth pursuing.

THE REFINEMENT DIALOGUE:
AN ELEGANT APPROACH TO REAL PROJECT GOALS, REFINED

Thanks to our stakeholder pathmap and our completed ToURspectives review, we can update who our primary stakeholders might be as well as prioritize whom we need to reach out to for clarifications or confirmations moving forward. We do this by respectfully revisiting with primary stakeholders and using a Pathoras-designed tool we call a **refinement dialogue**.

The refinement dialogue is essentially a conversation between our project team and each primary stakeholder. Using a series of open-ended and closed questions, our project teams confirm apparent needs and goals. We also broach the subject of the latent needs, obstacles, and goals we discovered while shadowing key stakeholders.

We then come to a consensus regarding the priority needs, obstacles, and goals that are required to address successful outcomes. We never underestimate the importance of a proper debriefing and the opportunity to have productive conversations with our customers.

Our refinement dialogues are a lot like the kinds of conversations that arise when a family embarks on a kitchen-remodeling experience. We're like kitchen designers: We listen to what the whole family wants in their kitchen and, based upon the primary cook in the family, help them build the most functional kitchen possible. We discuss what colors, designs, and styles they like. But as remodelers, we highlight other areas for consideration they may not have thought about. And if the majority of the family asks for trash receptacles near the kitchen sink, that's an efficiency trend that may benefit the whole family.

We are refining our—as well as the stakeholder's—understanding of all the project's goals. We once, for example, had a client call this dialogue a "refined dance." Like a ballroom waltz, we work together with the client to refine the project's end goals, so we're never stepping on one another's toes, all moving forward in the project in harmonious step.

We consider refinement dialogues to be invaluable to a project's success. They are opportunities for us to do three things above all else: (1) confirm our understanding of our customers' needs, (2) discuss the results of our ToURspectives review, and (3) outline the most vital project goals. We typically have a different set of questions for each primary stakeholder to ensure that our project team is getting proper clarification on what needs, obstacles, and goals are most important to that stakeholder.

There are several valuable approaches to a refinement dialogue. The first is to provide the customer with some of the observations we've gleaned while shadowing stakeholders. We tend to say things like, "When I was shadowing X, I noticed Y and Z." These observations are meant to either confirm our customers' apparent needs and goals or broach the subject of latent needs and goals we've discovered while shadowing.

Second, we sometimes also ask questions like, "And how about X?" or "Have you considered Y?" as it allows our customers to broaden their perspectives. We had one client say it was this approach that singlehandedly changed her entire outlook on the project. She had never thought about some of the trends we uncovered that could potentially benefit her team moving forward.

Third, we come to a consensus with the client regarding project goals; then we reiterate our understanding of their businesses or some key aspects of their process. It's all about listening and ensuring we are all on the same page. By using phrases like "So what I heard you say is X," or "Please correct us if we misunderstood, but our understanding of this process's need, obstacle, or goal is Z," it ensures we are all aligned with a common purpose before continuing.

We also ask our stakeholders questions like, "Based upon this conversation, would you say that Y is critical to project success?" Here it's critical that we ask "yes and no" questions. This allows us to confirm the apparent and latent needs and goals we've discovered, especially if the plan of action has been tweaked since the beginning of the project.

USING REFINEMENT DIALOGUES TO IDENTIFY LATENT NEEDS, OBSTACLES, AND GOALS AND DISCOVER REAL PROJECT GOALS

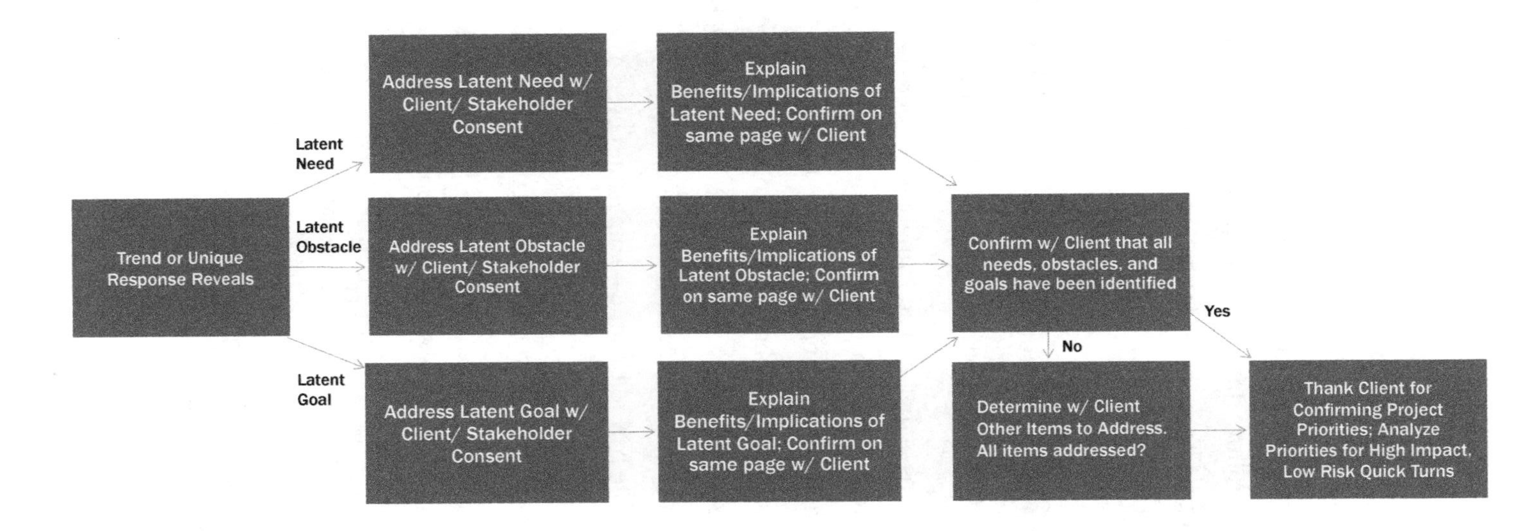

Even though every refinement dialogue is tailored for each primary stakeholder, we're providing an example of a refinement dialogue in flow chart form that often proves successful. This particular dialogue works especially well when we've uncovered latent needs, obstacles, and goals critical to refining what real project success should be for the project.

We follow the flow diagram to ask our client about each latent need, obstacle, or goal that has been discovered during our time with the stakeholders.

THE IMPORTANCE OF EMBEDDING:

SHADOWS THAT SHINE, FOR GREAT PROJECT GAIN

Embedding—that is, shadowing stakeholders—is such a critical tool in the Relevance Path it deserves to be highlighted. This is one instance where a shadow is the star. Why? Because shadowing stakeholders plays a key role in enhancing our understanding of real project needs, obstacles, and goals. Our greatest successes have been a direct result of having our project teams embedded in our customers' offices for a discernible period of time—sometimes even a year or more.

Sometimes customers worry about timelines, insisting they can't wait a year for results. We understand those concerns, and yet there are many advantages, both in terms of cost savings and efficiencies, in taking the time necessary to gain context about our customers, project needs, stakeholders, and office dynamics.

When we talk with our personnel at Pathoras, many can't recall projects in their own careers when they were able to come in cold and immediately craft a solution. They had to embed themselves within an office, learning the business and personnel dynamics, and earn the team's trust. This further refined their understanding of the "as is" state, which in turn helped us all reach the best "to be" state. Only then were they able to become extremely effective.

And to learn the best "to be" state, it's important that we engage with all the stakeholders.

As an example, let's look at IT projects. On many IT projects we've been asked to remediate, we have found that senior managers met with developers to outline specs and requirements or create a proposed IT system improvement. And yet they often neglected to speak with the people who were actually using the technologies. Overlooking users and stakeholders often negatively impacts the probability of success.

In every instance where Pathoras personnel have connected an IT team with an end user, we've gotten a much clearer understanding of latent obstacles.

Unfortunately, we see many projects fail because they don't take the time to shadow. Some agile development projects use their design and planning meetings to also communicate with the client. Design meetings (or even large stakeholder meetings) are not the right venue for relating and gleaning key information.

We take the time to engage and shadow users because (a) they're stakeholders, and (b) we want to make sure we connect with actual users. We conduct regular user group sessions to obtain feedback on functionality as our solutions are being developed (which we'll discuss much more in the "Execute" chapter and step of RELEVANCE, as this ensures project relevancy and further validates our proposed project path to the stakeholders).

One client, Bob H., calls embedding a "café style" approach, as he's asked developers to sit directly with analysts and learn their workflows and processes. It's a tactic Bob himself has successfully used to build high-impact systems for the military and national security presence overseas.

The proof is in the pudding. Every time Pathoras personnel have embedded and shadowed stakeholders, the end product has been positive, whether it's enabled process efficiencies and workflow efficiencies; saved our mission partners' time, resources, and money; or led a customer to become more productive in their daily processes. It's all because we were able to embed.

We recognize this approach is not always possible and that there are often time and budget constraints, but it's critical to grasp all the subtleties in a project. Think about the time it takes to shadow, enhance understanding of processes, identify the stakeholder pathmap, and revisit with key stakeholders to confirm agreement on apparent and latent needs, obstacles, and goals. Depending upon the size of the project, this could take a decent amount of time to accomplish. Beyond the reasons that we've already discussed in this chapter, there are many auxiliary benefits to embedding and engaging with our customer, in that they always enhance everyone's understandings of the project needs.

With a timetable of around a year, the project team understands—and I stress "truly understands"—needs and dynamics as well as what is and what is not possible in regard to money, time, and external relationships. It's only after these longer-term interactions, engagements, and shadowing that a well-oiled team and strong customer relationships emerge. Only then can we walk in concert with our customers and overcome false leads or red herrings. Had we not worked together with our customers and stakeholders to truly understand one another, we could have fallen into unforeseen pitfalls and wasted precious resources. The project would be a shadow of a different kind, one that's a faint representation of the project's true potential. Project costs, time, money, and resources spent would far eclipse what would have been saved had the project used tools from this Enhance and Visualize step to have a more relevant project outcome.

CHAPTER 4 KEY TAKEAWAYS

Long-term engagement creates massive insights that help overcome project problems. If you make a concerted effort to enhance and refine your understanding of the project by embedding with your client and stakeholders, the positive results are exponential. Your project will not only account for apparent needs, obstacles, and goals, but you will be able to discover the latent and real ones for project success. The return on investment for a project almost always balloons as a result of the time invested in the Enhance and Visualize phase of the Relevance Path.

- **Embedding** is a series of actions (shadowing, conducting enhancement dialogues, revisiting the success threshold review) in the Enhance and Visualize step of the Relevance Path, where the project team is afforded the opportunity to engage with customers and stakeholders and refine apparent and latent needs, obstacles, and goals for project success.
- **Apparent needs** are identified by the customer, which the customer believes have to occur in order to complete a given goal.
- **Latent needs** are hidden need requirements identified by discovering real end goals; such hidden needs and goals are only revealed by investing time with the customer to understand the customer's true situation and needed solution.
- **Apparent goals** are identified by the customer; they are what the customer believes need to be completed to meet an objective.
- **Latent goals** are hidden goals (end state requirements) identified by discovering real end goals; such unearthed goals are only revealed by investing time with the customer to understand the customer's true situation and needed solution.

- **Apparent obstacles** are obstacles identified by the customer, which the customer perceives to have played a role in preventing project objectives from being met.
- **Latent obstacles** are hidden obstacles that will prevent a client from meeting the latent project needs and latent project goals discovered through the Enhancement process.
- **Enhancement dialogue** is a series of questions the project team asks customers and stakeholders, where all of the information from the dialogue will be incorporated into proposed project solutions. The intention of the enhancement dialogue is to expand upon the project teams' initial engagement dialogue with customers and stakeholders and to build upon the rapport the project team established with a stakeholder during the Engage and Listen step. This dialogue further refines the project team's understanding of the products, atmospherics, and dynamics of the project's objectives, as well as the people and processes that surround it.
- **Stakeholder pathmap** is a visual identification of the stakeholder, their stakeholder types (primary, secondary, or tertiary), and the relationships between all stakeholders. This helps identify the type of relationships (financial, information, procedural, influential, approver, etc.) in play on a given project as well as interdependencies between stakeholders.
- **Enhancement trends or Unique Responses (E-ToURspectives) review** is an internal process review that plots all responses from the enhancement dialogues and shadowing sessions in order to identify trends (questions multiple stakeholders answered the same) and unique responses that merit further review, as well as the implications of those trends and unique responses. The ToURspectives review enables a visual representation of the trends

identified by specific stakeholders. It also identifies latent needs, obstacles, and goals that weren't known previously but were able to be discerned from reviewing enhancement dialogues from a critical mass perspective.

- **ToURspectives visuals** are visual representations of impactful statistics and results of the ToURspectives review combined with visually identifying ToURspectives implications and latent needs, obstacles, and goals. The ToURspectives visuals incorporate calculated percentages of how stakeholders feel about a topic and provide the information in a quick, easily digestible way to stakeholders.
- **A refinement dialogue** is a conversation between the project team and each primary stakeholder that highlights observations, trends, and unique responses (as well as the implications) gleaned while shadowing stakeholders. Using a series of open-ended and closed questions, the project team confirms with the primary stakeholders the apparent needs and goals, broaches the subject of the latent needs and goals discovered while shadowing, and confirms the priority needs, obstacles, and goals to address for project success.

CHAPTER

FIVE

The Analyze Step: Identifying Low-Risk, Low-Cost, High-Return Quick Wins and Pinpointing Long-Term Beneficial and Unbiased Relevant Project Solutions

Do not be led by others, awaken your own mind, amass your own experience, and decide for yourself your own path.

—The Atharva Veda

MAIN POINTS:

- Establishing and revisiting a solution's relevance (through the **Solution Relevance Review**) prevents requirements/scope creep from overtaking real project goals and keeps the project on the success target to identify viable options for a strong project ROI.
- Tools (such as the **Quick Wins Risk Analysis** and **Q-ToUR-spectives Review**) reveal quick wins and mini-solutions based on low-risk, low-cost, and high-return initiatives that can remove project pain points.

- Understanding behavioral economics and psychological phenomena, such as the **stereotype bias**, further prevents project objectives from becoming clouded in biased (and costly) ways.

Every year my husband, Andy, and his family take an annual pilgrimage to the Outer Banks, a yearly vacation ritual I've come to love myself. The Outer Banks is a charming sliver of land off the coast of North Carolina which is lined by a beach nearly 100 miles long that regularly welcomes a steady onslaught of Atlantic Ocean waves.

Although my husband has been going there for 40 years, he still finds himself facing the same problems he did when he was a kid of trying to endure the often-searing direct sunlight. He has one umbrella that, by some miracle, has weathered all 40 years of his travels. It's a rusted old thing that has been affectionately called Trusty Rusty. No other umbrellas or tents have survived even a week in the Outer Banks. The only downside is that Trusty Rusty is small. It'll only shade two people at max, leaving the rest of our family melting in the sun.

In previous years, we always wound up buying a new umbrella (or for that matter, a tent), never bothering to do any research. And without fail, they always broke on us, which was a very costly and frustrating expense. We always left the beach sunburned, looking like a family of red lobsters.

So finally, a few years ago, we wised up and spent some time evaluating possible solutions. Should we buy a half tent? A fair tent? An umbrella that we could attach to the ground? We were stumped as to which one to choose, as there were a lot of factors that we needed to consider—variables that only became evident once we started our evaluation.

And so we began to *analyze* our options. We learned more about different materials, SPF cloth ratings, wind support, and the need for galvanized metals to counteract the salty air. After much research, we found a strong fiberglass-pole umbrella that was the right choice. It's been a keeper, having endured the unforgiving conditions of the Outer Banks for a number of years now.

What had been an expensive and frustrating yearly quest to find a short-term fix has turned into a long-term solution that's proven to be both beneficial and economical for all of us. We are officially red lobsters no more!

Our days of getting burned by the sun were done. But sadly at Pathoras, that wasn't the case; we often saw clients get burned themselves before we supported them because they made the very same mistakes my husband and I did for years. They wasted valuable time and resources by not taking the time to step back and analyze the source of their problems.

It's possible to prevent your burns from ever occurring. How? By using tools in our Analyze step of RELEVANCE. When we analyze a client's project, what we're really trying to do is establish a smart course of action based upon real project root causes. We're trying to identify quick efficiency enablers, as well as lay out potential successful long-term solutions. In essence, we're providing our clients with a number of potential pathways to reach their real intended goals. We're providing a set of options. Ultimately, the decision on which pathway to travel is entirely up to the client.

When we analyze a project, we're also looking at the psychological pitfalls that can lead a project astray. Our emphasis on identifying and correcting hidden problems is one of the reasons that our RELEVANCE methodology has an unrivaled track record for ensuring both known project goals and unanticipated ones are met in a variety of fields. Our methodology has proven advantageous in finding success in everything from project and change management to business processes to workflow management and IT practices.

This chapter provides tools for how—and why—projects should be analyzed and how we craft potential solutions for overcoming project hurdles. In the end, the Analyze step, coupled with our deep understanding of behavioral economics, acts as a compass in helping our clients stay on the correct path toward achieving relevant solutions.

PAIN POINTS:
HOW THEY CAN BE GOOD FOR THE PROJECT AT LARGE

This much is certain: If you're on an overgrown nature "trail," how can you possibly see where you're going? You stumble into poison ivy that you didn't even realize was there or a poisonous spider lurking in a bush. Unforeseen obstacles will make your trip that much more difficult, and you'll be less likely to reach your destination. But if you knew what poison ivy or that spider looked like, and knew how to counteract it, you'd be able to avoid those pitfalls and reach your destination poison-free, not to mention much more quickly, too.

We see the proverbial poison ivy or spider situations every day when we work with clients. They represent pain points which prevent our clients from performing their best work. Some arrive in the form of painful manual processes, others are laborious duplicative activities, and yet others are marked by a lack of structured workflows that impedes communication and scalability. We discover these pain points with our tools such as enhancement dialogues and shadowing (as we discussed in chapter 4). In this Analyze step, we reveal the tools that enable pain points to become great opportunities for quick wins.

Here's why: When it comes to the Analyze step, the Relevance Path is designed to identify and address a client's pain points and potential pitfalls. Not addressing either of these traps inevitably leads to problems down the road, whether it's frustrated personnel who are unable to accomplish tasks or focused employees who lack the necessary organizational workflows or technologies to get the job done correctly. Whenever resentment builds in a project, it can often snowball, forcing clients to either lose motivation or avoid meeting their primary goals. At Pathoras, we believe in rooting out resentment before it takes hold.

By alleviating the stress of pain points through building quick wins, we can help identify both latent and real needs, obstacles, and goals. It helps us to identify if there are any new needs, obstacles, or goals that have arisen since we implemented our quick wins. Oftentimes there are, which helps pave the way toward new destinations our customers never thought possible.

FROM PAIN POINTS TO QUICK WINS: HOW TO MAKE LEMONADE OUT OF LEMONS WITH QUICK WINS TOOLS

We look at pain points as a means to an end. They can be critical bittersweet ingredients that impede a project's success. Pain points are like lemons, a key ingredient in a delicious lemonade recipe that quick wins can produce.

We work on identifying, analyzing, and implementing "quick wins," which we define as high-return, low-risk mini-solutions (our lemonade) that get a project out of a rut and begin to build momentum. Sometimes when a client becomes too frustrated, they simply don't have the energy to call it a priority any longer. Or they're so frustrated that they can't prioritize appropriately either.

So earning a few quick wins is a fast and easy way to build credibility and rapport with a client, and quick wins often do something far more profound.

Frequently, converting paint points (lemons) to succulent quick-win lemonade is a key step in identifying latent and real needs, obstacles, or goals that may have been overlooked for the project writ large. This can occur when a client's highest priority (or highest return) pain point(s) obstruct a project's forward momentum. Quick wins typically solve an initial problem and help project frustration dissolve to some degree. Thus, they help uncover the real issues that have stalled the project. Eliminating key pain points allows us to then address real project goals.

All too often we find our clients trapped in what we refer to, within Pathoras, as a state of "**stuckocation**."

Stuckocation is that point in a project when you feel so stuck that things begin to feel suffocating. Stuck plus suffocation equals stuckocation. Oftentimes these problems are the result of other projects that a client is working on, inefficient processes that lead to unimpressive results, or inept technologies that are supposed to help people but in reality they don't. They're pain points.

Whatever the cause, stuckocation always involves a feeling of despair and frustration. And as we all know all too well, and suggested above, frustration rarely leads to productivity. So rather than deliver one complete product, which we've often seen go past deadline and fail to address actual goals, we start small. We develop interim processes to help productivity and workflow and then show the stakeholders the potential benefits.

To counteract a nasty bout of stuckocation, here's our "lemons into lemonade" recipe for making efficient and effective quick wins. We make the teams we are working with or their processes (1) more effective, (2) more efficient, or (3) both. We consider anything outside of achieving greater efficiencies and greater effectiveness as ancillary goals. We're absolutely convinced that the farther a solution strays from its core mission, the more nebulous—not to mention costly and inefficient—a project becomes.

Here's how we establish the right quick wins for scrumptious, thirst-quenching lemonade:

- We assign field team members to address areas of opportunity for quick efficiencies.
- We analyze the results of the *E-ToURspectives reviews* (discussed in chapter 4), building upon the information we received from our customers in their refinement dialogue.
- We look at the risks of implementing a quick win (in a Quick Wins Risk Analysis) and only implement low-risk, low-cost, high-return quick wins.
- We build quick wins according to the needs, real needs, obstacles, and goals of our primary and secondary stakeholders.

So what we're really doing is prioritizing project needs based upon stakeholder feedback with primary stakeholders obviously having the highest priorities. What problems must be addressed first? Which are tertiary? Answering these questions helps us to define proposed quick-wins options and plug them into our **Quick-Wins Risk Analysis.**

In our quick-wins risk analysis, we identify potential risks associated with each possible solution. We identify the type of risk, whether it's related to policies or to system, personnel, political, or office dynamics. We also identify the consequences of that risk, and what events will happen if that risk occurs. Then we analyze the risk associated with each mini solution so we can determine the best course of action to implement a mitigation strategy. A quick-win solution with low-risk impact and a high probability of success are the ones we immediately begin implementing.

This is why we not only identify, discuss, and implement quick wins but also review the effectiveness of these quick wins. We implement only the highest-ranking quick-win options and obtain feedback on them by employing what we call our **Quick Wins Trends or Unique Responses** (aka **Q-ToURspectives**) Review. This approach is very similar to what we do during our E-ToURspectives review (that we discussed in chapter 4), but this time we focus on the quick wins that will benefit the project at large by being implemented.

An example of a Quick Wins ToURspectives Review can be found at therelevancepath.com

It's here in the Q-ToURspectives review that we typically uncover real project needs, obstacles, or goals, since the quick wins address pain points clouding critical needs or goals.

That being said, developing quick wins are not the ultimate goal. Quick wins are the equivalent of stringing a few first downs together. They're nice and important, but in the end, it's getting the ball in the end zone and putting points on the board that separates successful projects from unsuccessful ones. Quick wins build confidence and yield unforeseen efficiencies. Small successes lead to greater gains. Confidence breeds confidence. And the next thing you know, a nearly forgotten or disenfranchised project is generating energy, momentum, and newfound excitement throughout an organization.

CASE STUDY:

DELIVERING HIGH-RETURN, LOW-COST QUICK WINS THROUGH SHADOWING AND RELATIONSHIP BUILDING

Sometimes merely observing a project in action isn't enough. More often, in order to properly diagnose what is stalling a project, we need to embed (as discussed in chapter 4) one of our Pathorians inside a particular project. During one particularly time-sensitive project, for example, one of our specialists flew overseas to obtain a firsthand perspective on what our client was facing.

In this particular project, time was of the essence, as it included an expensive and long-term proposal to completely revamp a large logistic center's software. The client's logistic center was suffering from a significant productivity problem. The center was properly staffed but couldn't seem to keep up with its workload. And our client couldn't pinpoint how to create new efficiencies.

Fortunately, our Pathorian was able to identify the key logjam by doing something very simple. He spent time with the people who were actually doing the work. He ate with them in their cafeteria, grabbed dinner with them at local fast-food spots, and then went back with them for their evening shift. In doing so, he noticed the client's people were hamstrung by having to work on single 14-inch screens.

By being on the ground, he realized that the center also had many seventeen-inch monitors that were not being used. Thus, distributing dual seventeen-inch monitors onto existing desks provided a low-risk, high-return quick win. The analysis also revealed it could be done in just two days and would significantly increase productivity at little to no cost. And it did just that. The logistics center didn't have to expend capital (upwards of $200,000) to upgrade its software. The office was able to make huge strides with few resources just by taking the time to carefully analyze the situation in full, rather than opting for the more costly solution, which involved implementing software to dual-screen information on the 14-inch screens. This allowed for productivity to soar and meet the office's workload needs: the project's actual goal.

In another highly successfully project, one of our Pathorians outlined the need for quicker turnaround from an external office. His office was having difficulty incentivizing the external office to process requests more quickly. He took the time to discuss the motivations behind the customers' frustrations and realized responsiveness was sluggish at best.

This negatively impacted the team's ability to support real-time operational needs. Not only did the external office lack the knowledge necessary to provide timely responses, they lacked the ability to provide relevant responses. Our Pathorian used his IT background to design and develop a quick in-house system. The system not only highlighted mission-relevant information, but the system completed in two hours requests which previously took an average of fourteen days to wait for an external office to triage. This resulted in a 16,700 percent productivity increase in established real-time relevant mission support to the field, which dropped the time it took for each job from fourteen days of waiting to just two hours. The team could then support real-time, mission-critical operational needs—what really mattered to the team and the downstream consumers.

PAVING THE WAY TO MACRO SOLUTIONS:
THE SOLUTIONS RELEVANCE REVIEW

Now that we've cleared the overgrown trail by using our quick wins tools (analyzing and implementing low-risk, high-return quick wins), we can really analyze the possible ways forward to our final project destination. This is because we've conducted the Q-ToURspectives review and identified any other needs, obstacles, or goals, so we can move on to a discussion of macro goals. We zero in on the project writ large and conduct a **Solutions Relevance Review.** For many projects, the Solution Relevance Review is a great tool to use in tandem with all of our Quick Wins tools.

Similar to the *Quick Wins Risk Analysis*, our Solutions Relevance Review focuses specifically on potential solutions and their associated risk levels. If a solution's features are considered a higher risk for a project's success, we outline how to mitigate those risks.

In the Solutions Relevance Review, we ask a series of questions that include:

- What is the customer's time line?
- Is it flexible or rigid?
- What is the customer's priority, time, or budget?
- What are the primary stakeholders' real needs, obstacles, and goals?
- What are the secondary stakeholders' real needs, obstacles, and goals?
- Do any of the stakeholders' project requirements pertain to all stakeholder types? The project at large?

When we look at risk, we consider the following factors:

- Risk type: project costs, project schedule, performance, policy, system, personnel, political/office dynamics
- Risk potential: potential to impact project costs, project schedule, or performance:
    - High: great potential
    - Medium: slight potential
    - Low: relatively little potential

- Risk probability: Probability of occurring:
    - High: greater than 70 percent chance of occurring
    - Medium: 30 – 69 percent chance of occurring
    - Low: less than 30 percent chance of occurring

Our Solutions Relevance Review allows us to analyze the real needs, obstacles, and goals (the real project requirements) that our customized solutions address, as well as which ones they don't address. We create a matrix of potential solutions so we can visually see which solutions address most of the real project requirements for each of the primary, secondary, and tertiary stakeholders.

As we meld our potential solution sets, we blend these questions with solutions that will address the real goals identified with RELEVANCE tools, such as the *refinement dialogues*, the *E-ToUR-spectives review* (both discussed in chapter 4), and the *Q-ToURspectives review*. We can then create an essential macro view of the most relevant solution options for project success.

BEHAVIORAL ECONOMICS AND PSYCHOLOGY:

WHY THEY'RE POWERFUL FOR CRAFTING RELEVANT SOLUTIONS AND OVERCOMING TYPICAL PROJECT PITFALLS

I've always believed solutions aren't primarily about the technologies or innovations behind them, but rather the people behind them. It's people, after all, who piece the solutions together and build the trusted relationships needed to make any solution succeed. They are the engines that identify and create relevant solution sets. It's our ability to infuse a human touch into projects while creating solutions that are relevant to our customers' real needs that is one of our greatest differentiators.

We often see a variety of project pitfalls that could be overcome simply if biases were taken into account (since they aren't, most of the time).

Sadly, most project teams do not understand their client and stakeholders' daily processes, pain points, or daily motivation. It's even rarer to find a project team that understands a client's mission or business objectives, let alone why clients conduct the processes and employ the people they do. We also find that project teams frequently misinterpret clients' needs and goals, especially the rationale behind those assumed needs and goals.

In projects we've worked on that involved system design and development, we've come to find that, oftentimes, most developers who support project teams are biased toward the developmental frameworks they know best. They therefore see a client's requirements through very specific filters, or they determine a client's needs based on what they did during their last successful project.

We've also found, time and again, that intuitive systems and process designs are not universal. Development teams will often create systems that look aesthetically attractive but force analysts to scroll through five screens just to find the information they need. Such designs are counterintuitive and counterproductive.

All of these tendencies are detrimental to a project's success and will all nearly guarantee the creation of a big fat relevance gap (as discussed in chapter 2). These tendencies are, in many ways, why we created our Relevance Path in the first place. It's our belief that teams should stay focused on crafting relevant, efficient, and productive solutions that address the real needs, obstacles, and goals that a client hopes to achieve—and not be influenced by personal biases.

This is why we consider behavioral economics and psychological decision-making phenomena to be so important. Only by understanding the psychological underpinnings of a given situation can we focus intently on our client's environment and end goals. Quite frankly, it's the only way to develop relevant solutions. Clients come to Pathoras because they have a custom need and know we'll work to customize a solution to meet that particular need.

Our ability to work with managers and tailor our solutions to best support their management style is only one of many ways we support our clients differently than the majority of the project teams out there. It's yet another layer of our human touch and how we leverage behavioral economics and psychology to build trust in relationships and strong solutions as well as overcome common project pitfalls.

ERASING THE IRRATIONAL: OVERCOMING STEREOTYPE BIAS TO ENSURE REAL PROJECT GOALS SUCCEED

Having supported the national security arena for decades, we've had to learn how to provide continuity and consistent support in an ever-changing and fluid industry. We know what it is to love and be dedicated to a mission, just like our clients. So we know how to quickly develop a one-team, one-fight approach to help our clients achieve their core missions.

For the term of our engagement, we are a part of that agency, customer, organization, partner, or company. Our goal is to ensure their real goals are achieved. We do this is by zeroing in on the irrational factors in human decision-making. This is a core concept of behavioral economics, one that stems from the fact that humans don't always make rational decisions. Humans sometimes make decisions that are not intuitive and don't make sense. Some of these irrational decisions stem from cognitive biases that humans have.

At Pathoras, we often find some form of a bias presents itself, either within a project team or with a stakeholder. This is why it's so important to be aware of these biases so we can identify them as they come up and work to overcome them. This is a unique difference between RELEVANCE and other project change management, business process, or IT framework operations.

So here we'll begin our discussion of biases by looking at something called a **stereotype bias**, which is our collective tendency as humans to be swayed by people who appear authoritative on topics we're not familiar with. Whether it's showing resistance to conflict or a willingness to accept initial information on the topic, it's common to easily accept concepts presented on topics we know little about.

Unfortunately, the initial information humans absorb about a particular topic is also the most rudimentary information about that same subject, which in many cases turns out to be stereotypical information. And sadly, consciously or subconsciously, stereotypes largely affect the beliefs and preferences of decision makers, purchasers, and customers.

Think about the stereotype bias this way.

Let's say you're under the weather; you're just not feeling right. What's the first thing many of us do? We go to our ever-trustworthy friend, the Internet. We type in our symptoms. Within minutes, we self-diagnose ourselves. We assume we know what our illness is. Why? Because we've read about some symptom that commonly points back to a particular diagnosis.

But is that assumption, in fact, the right diagnosis? Women rarely have chest pains when they're having a heart attack. In fact women may have heartburn instead, but that's not common knowledge. A chest-clutching pain is what we expect, which provides more proof that we often trust information that's commonly perceived or easy to digest.

Oftentimes a customer's beliefs have been formed from popular and public sentiment, which may be the result of common stereotypes. We've worked with a lot of clients who have heard about a new product or tool. Just because it's being used by others, they automatically think they need it.

For example, many of our clients assumed that the cloud is the answer for all computer security problems. Yet it, too, has security ramifications and isn't the best choice for every project.

In fact, we were once asked by a client to implement a multilevel user functionality within a cloud environment. The clients said that they wanted cloud functionality, and by doing so, they believed all functionality would almost magically become instantly secured against hackers. What the customer did not understand was that in order to develop and operate in a secure, relevant functionality, Pathoras personnel needed to establish use-case scenarios, user roles, and code based upon current updates. In the end, it took time to educate our customer on security ramifications and necessities as well as the role-based user functionalities needed to protect information on the cloud.

The client's belief that the cloud could cure all of its problems inhibited the organization from truly understanding the project's maximum potential. That is, until Pathoras personnel worked with them to break down the stereotypes, explain in a user-friendly way how the technology works, and help create a plan best suited to get them where they wanted to go.

In a day and age when "cloud," "cyber," and "big data" buzzwords are overhyped, the overuse of these terms can lead to dangerous over-generalizations for nontechnical customers. Customers in any market have preconceived notions and preferences surrounding solution ideas. This often leads to the development of a product or process that falls short of meeting critical needs and goals. Furthermore, it is often based upon the stereotype bias. This only adds fuel to an already difficult-to-solve relevance gap.

We see it as our mission to overcome biases in every project we work on, helping clients emerge with solutions that yield long-term dividends and results.

CHAPTER 5 KEY TAKEAWAYS

Project teams and organizations can prevent requirements creep from happening by identifying viable options for solutions, all based on real project goals that can be revealed after eliminating project pain points. This can happen by analyzing pain points from a risk perspective, where you can then reveal low-risk, low-cost, and high-return quick wins and mini project solutions. You can also further discover the right project solutions by keeping in mind behavioral economics and psychological phenomena, such as the stereotype bias, when analyzing and crafting project solutions.

- **Quick Wins** are high-return, low-risk mini-solutions that get a project out of a rut and begin to build momentum.
- **Stuckocation** is that point in a project when an individual, team, or organization feels so stuck that events begin to feel suffocating, often the result of an overwhelming number of problems, issues, or projects that a client is working. Inefficient processes lead to unimpressive results or inept technologies that are "supposed" to help people but in reality they don't. "Stuck" plus "suffocation" equals "stuckocation."
- **Quick Wins Risk Analysis** is the identification of potential risks associated with each possible quick-win solution. These include the type of risk (whether it's related to policy or system, personnel, or political/office dynamics), the actual project risk, the consequences of that risk (what events will happen if that risk occurs), or the risk associated with each solution set. The goal is to identify the best course of action to minimize any risk and implement a mitigation strategy as well as identify quick wins that are low-risk, low-cost, and high return on investment.

- **Quick Wins Trends and Unique Responses (a.k.a. Q-ToUR-spectives) Review** seeks to identify, discuss, and implement quick wins and review the effectiveness of these quick wins (from an overall trend or unique perspective) in order to help identify both latent and real needs, obstacles, and goals as well as identify if there are any new needs, obstacles, or goals that have arisen since we implemented the quick wins.
- A **Solutions Relevance Review** focuses on the project writ large and creates a matrix of potential solution sets and their associated risk levels while analyzing the real needs, obstacles, and goals that each new solution addresses. This helps clients visually see which solutions address most of the real needs, obstacles, and goals for each of the primary, secondary, and tertiary stakeholders, as well as which real needs, obstacles, and goals aren't addressed.
- **Stereotype Bias** is our human tendency to be swayed by people who appear authoritative on topics that individuals, teams, or organizations are not familiar with, resulting in readily accepting concepts presented on new topics that an individual, team, or organization knows little about, whether those concepts are accurate or not.

CHAPTER

SIX

The Numerate Step: Overcoming Project Risks and Depicting Project Value

Unexplored paths lead to undiscovered treasures.

—Constance Chuks Friday

MAIN POINTS:

- Risk plays a role in projects and has to be evaluated and numerated to reveal the best project solutions; it's the project team's job to proactively identify the risks as well as ways to mitigate or avoid them.
- A **Solutions Valuation Review** ensures the project team understands the benefits (and risks) of choosing a specific solution or solutions and also serves as a control mechanism to issue updated project benefits, schedules, risk, and budget plans. These are often based upon a past-present-future perspective of solution sets.

- A **Relevant Solutions Pathmap** depicts each potential project solution's corresponding benefits and risks in a digestible way so stakeholders can easily determine their preferred project solutions.
- Identifying **stakeholder value types** and **value profiles** ensures project benefits are communicated to stakeholders according to what matters most to them.
- Remaining cognizant of phenomena such as the **status quo bias**, **loss aversion**, and **change blindness** is critical in accurately evaluating project benefits and outcomes for the best project solutions.

Every year at Pathoras, we conduct several surveys that provide a sense of how we're meant to best support the Pathoras team, their needs, obstacles, and goals. At other organizations, surveys are mere formalities. Employees begrudgingly fill them out, annoyed that they have to waste time on questions that seldom lead to tangible improvements.

But at Pathoras, most of our people actually look forward to filling out our surveys because each review is designed to elicit honest feedback on important professional issues, including how well we are supporting Pathorians in terms of compensation, benefits, time off, training, mentorship, career advancement opportunities, work/life balance, team cohesion, corporate strategy, and most interesting of all, professional fulfillment.

Although I wait with bated breath each year to see the results of these surveys, there's a part of me that pushes away any apprehension that I might be harboring because I'm secure in the knowledge that only good can come out of knowing more about how our team members feel about Pathoras. The truth of the matter is that I want desperately to know—whether good or bad—what our team feels about our benefits, processes, and communication. If they are satisfied, I'm relieved. But should they voice uncertainty, I know that we can revisit their concerns and then adjust our processes for the better.

Over the years Pathoras has had the honor of winning many awards, including *Inc.*'s 50 Best Small and Midsize Workplaces in the United States and *Silicon Review*'s Top 50 Workplaces as well as *Washington Business Journal*'s Best Places to Work. I attribute these honors to the openness and sense of candor that are embedded in our surveys and our culture, all of which stem from the belief that we should place the greatest importance on the values held by our employees.

Once we have identified our team's values, we can discover new ways to support our Pathoras family members and retain the team values that are central to everything we do. Since value is at the heart of everything we do at Pathoras, it's only natural that value propositions are at the heart of the Relevance Path as well. We ask questions throughout our RELEVANCE methodology that help us cater to our customers' and stakeholders' individual value profiles.

It's here during the numerate step that we evaluate potential solution sets by what our clients value, and what they value most. It's here that we provide the *why* behind our solutions—*why* our solutions will lead to great productivity, cost savings, or process efficiencies. These are, after all, solutions that address whatever is most valued by our customers.

This is also the phase when we identify the resources needed to put these solution paths into action as well as those that can be better utilized. Our primary aim is to identify impasses that may be impeding success while paving a course to reach our destination, wherever that end goal lies.

But it's not enough to simply stand before our customers and prattle on about value. We have a responsibility to show how value will be generated by our project solutions. First, we must begin by honing in on how each individual stakeholder defines the term "value."

VALUE TYPES:

SPEAKING WITH STAKEHOLDERS ABOUT PROJECT BENEFITS IN A LANGUAGE THEY UNDERSTAND

When we think of the term "value" we view it as the sum total of how a customer's business mission, objectives, and culture benefit from a project.

Although each and every client and stakeholder perceives value differently, there are certain **value types** that most of our clients seek.

IDENTIFYING VALUE TYPES AND PROFILES FOR BEST UNDERSTANDING CLIENT GOALS AND OBJECTIVES

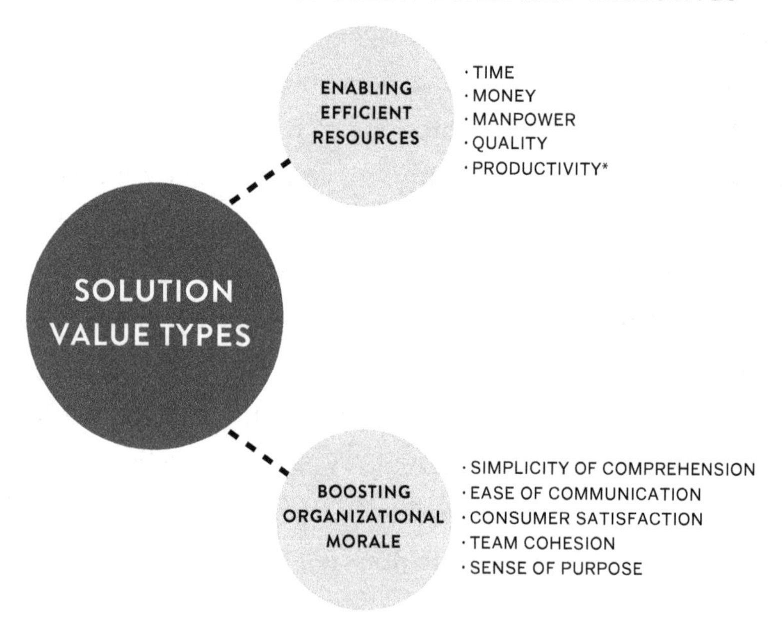

*PRODUCTIVITY, NOT QUANTITY IS USED HERE. QUANTITY IMPLIES INCREASE AT THE COST OF QUALITY. PRODUCTIVITY IS BETTER QUALITY AND QUANTITY.

Value types for each of our clients can (and typically do) include some or all of these values. The same is true for stakeholders. By understanding the value types for each client or stakeholder, we can create their corresponding value profiles.

For customers working in the field of national security, value is often defined as successfully completing particular mission objectives, whether it's creating team cohesion or protecting American interests. At a more micro level, our mission-forward customers also tend to see value in producing and disseminating reports for operators and their awareness—that is, productivity.

Our IT customers, by comparison, often see value in providing effective software and hardware infrastructure (time, manpower, user satisfaction), while commercial customers want to ensure that time, money, and manpower are efficiently utilized.

When working with research and development customers, we find that they tend to place value on creating innovative solutions in cutting-edge technologies to solve current problems even if it means that innovative discovery is not efficient at this point in time.

This is why it's important to identify the values each stakeholder perceives in addition to the stakeholder types (as explained in chapter 3). In this way, we can prioritize the value propositions and priorities based upon the stakeholder's type. We are then able to identify each customer and stakeholder's preferences and make sure we depict solution options in ways that benefit and matter most to customers and stakeholders.

By using a language that they personally speak, all stakeholders essentially get to view the project's value in a way that makes sense to them.

SOLUTIONS VALUATION REVIEW: REVEALING WHAT SOLUTIONS MAXIMIZE BENEFIT FOR PROJECT STAKEHOLDERS AND OVERALL PROJECT SUCCESS

It is important to understand how value is perceived by our primary, secondary and tertiary stakeholders, which is why we start identifying values in other steps of RELEVANCE. To ensure consistency in value profile, it's a best practice to review customer responses to the questions posed in the enhancement dialogues and refinement dialogues of the Enhance and Visualize step (chapter 4). In this way, we can see if value profiles remain consistent or change as we use different tools to move toward creating the best solution sets relative to what matters most to our customers and stakeholders.

And based upon the solution sets we identified in our solutions relevance review (chapter 5), we can now further translate values into our **Solutions Valuation Review**, where we gauge the value of each solution set according to specific stakeholder types.

An example of how to effectively use a Solutions Valuation Review can be found at therelevancepath.com.

Our solutions valuation review is based not only on how risky the potential solutions may be but also on the value profiles that our customers and stakeholders perceive. It's here that we ask another set of questions:

Who are the decision makers?

What do they value?

What are their value profiles?

Then we tailor the potential solutions to meet what the decision makers and stakeholders value. We can easily see what solutions provide the best benefit for our stakeholders (factoring in risk and risk mitigation) and what solutions will ensure our customers and stakeholders can meet and exceed project goals.

BEHAVIORAL ECONOMICS AND PSYCHOLOGY:

TOOLS THAT ENABLE EVALUATING PROJECT BENEFITS FOR THE BEST PROJECT SOLUTIONS

Just as we previously discussed stereotype biases in chapter 5, procedural biases are common as well. As we build our solution sets, we need to stay mindful of cognitive biases that sometimes bubble to the surface in working with our customers. We are all guilty of falling into predictable patterns, but knowing what these patterns are and how to overcome them inevitably gets us much closer to satisfying our customers' needs.

There are several key concepts to remember when it comes to biases. In 1979, Amos Tversky and future Nobel Prize winner Daniel Kahneman produced a hypothesis called prospect theory, which argued that people perceive as well as feel the effects of a loss more than a gain. As a result, people tend to make decisions that avoid potential losses, even if they can gain more by taking appropriate risk.

In essence, prospect theory is based upon the idea of **loss aversion**, a finding that helps to describe what actual gains are seen as losses. Ultimately people tend to focus on a loss versus a gain rather than the overall outcome of the decision.

Loss aversion is an important phenomenon to understand but is often lost on people because it can get complex rather quickly. So here's a simplified example with simplified odds to easily understand loss aversion.

Say we're in Vegas. We've been hitting roulette and pretty much coming out even, but now it's time to up the ante. If we bet $10, our odds are less than 20 percent to win $15. Or we can go to the blackjack table where we can bet $20 and have a slightly less than 50 percent chance of winning $75.

If we calculated the expected values of the bets (the amount of money we expected to win if we continue to place the same bet on the same odds) here's what we'd find: an expected value of losing $475 if we continue to take the $10 bet. But we'd have an expected value of winning $2,750 if we decided to take and continue to take the $20 bet. Many of us will choose to stick with roulette (or even hit the penny slots instead) because of loss aversion.

In our minds, we may see the $10 bet as only losing $10 even though our chances of winning $75 at blackjack are better if we bet the $20. The thought of losing that $20 blackjack bet overshadows the $75 we could gain; thus, we stick with the $10 bet since we perceive it to be less of a loss.

What prospect theory teaches us is that the biases we employ in Vegas don't always stay in Vegas. These biases often travel back home with us and creep not only into our daily lives but also into the way organizations approach projects.

Which is why at Pathoras, we believe it's critical for us to understand why customers make certain decisions on certain projects—whether that's a decision to continue a project in a specific way even when it's not performing well or, conversely, take a leap of faith and reformat a project in a new way.

How, you may ask, do we help customers avoid these loss aversion pitfalls? By pointing out where our customers can gain value and by demonstrating how that value can be customized to meet their goals and exceed any potential losses they envisioned.

CASE STUDY:

UNDERSTANDING VALUE TYPES TO OVERCOME LOSS AVERSION

We had a particularly memorable customer who was afraid to veer too far from the project's initial course because she feared the unknown. Yet it was an undeniable fact that the current course wasn't working. A complete lack of standardized processes was wreaking havoc on the office. There was no semblance of organization. Chaos reigned.

As a result, her team was very overworked, underappreciated, and in a perpetual state of turmoil as time-sensitive requests came in. The morale of the project's team members was, to put it mildly, in the dumps. As we talked with our client and asked her what motivated her to come to work every day, we began to formulate a value profile for her.

In time, we found that she fell squarely into a profile we call "boosting organization morale," which is built around the need for ease of communication, consumer satisfaction, and team cohesion. This very capable customer of ours simply didn't know how to move forward. Even though she always tried to keep her team's best interest at heart, she continually froze at the very thought of progress. We proposed several simple solutions, each tailored to address her value profile. To her, any change would be overwhelming and unproductive.

In the end, we were able to carefully navigate our client away from a point of stasis, which soon propelled the project forward with newfound speed and unanticipated efficiencies. These changes led to the creation of standardized operating procedures and identified points of contacts for areas of responsibility. Due to this approach, the team also quickly comprehended the solution because it was simple and clean. The team bonded. A team with clear responsibilities, after all, is a happier team.

Buoyed by a greater understanding of daily activities and the additional support provided thanks to a more defined organizational structure, the team experienced elevated levels of satisfaction with their work. As a result, our client overcame her fear of getting something wrong. What could have continued on as a disastrous project turned into an extremely successful one.

STATUS QUO BIAS:

OVERCOMING NEGATIVITY WITH A TIME-PHASED VIEW OF PROJECT BENEFIT

It's important to remember that there are more biases to consider than just loss aversion. We are also skilled in ferreting out something called **status quo bias**, which occurs when people perceive anything outside of the status quo as a loss. In these cases, change is always considered negative (like our client in the case study above). The phenomena may stem from the fact that most of us simply don't like change.

I have a friend, for example, who turned down a new position at her current job—one at a related "sister" office that offered more pay and greater opportunities for growth—simply because it necessitated change. She simply couldn't see past the change. To her, the forest wasn't beyond the trees. The forest was dark and dank. Heaven forbid she even attempt to walk in those woods. Even with all the benefits she could have accrued, the prospect of change spooked her because it, in essence, would be different from her current situation.

Although the status quo bias is an irrational preference for one's current situation, it is a cognitive bias that can be overturned and transformed into positive results. Here's why. It's also human nature for most of us to place greater emphasis on the more recent past than the distant past. This is not to say humans are forgetful. It's just that we tend to focus more on what's happened to us recently as opposed to something that happened a long time ago. In keeping this status quo phenomenon in mind, we focus on ensuring relevant past experiences are appropriately assessed and the right information is being utilized so that we can create the most ideal solutions possible.

In many cases, we've seen our primary POC in a client's organization leave to take a different position, so our new POCs don't typically know what happened in the past. That's just one reason why it's so important that we focus on offering a sense of the past, present, and future on every project we work on.

By doing so, we overcome status quo and loss aversion biases by showing our customers where they were in the past, where they are right now, and how our solutions will get them to where they want to be in the future. We focus on showing long-term value rather than just the short-term benefits of technological upgrades or newfangled kitschy tools.

By focusing on the value of a solution, we're able to understand how a customer can identify the negatives of a situation while also helping them see the real needs, obstacles, and goals that are addressed in each proposed solution. In this way, we can best ensure that the big-picture positives of any solution designed will shine through.

CHANGE FOR CHANGE'S SAKE: COMBATING CHANGE BLINDNESS WITH VISIONS FOR SUCCESS

We make it a point to present our solutions in a way that reduces the potential for what we call change blindness. ***Change blindness*** is a phenomenon in which people are so unaware of their surroundings that real changes in their environment often go completely unnoticed.

How many times, for example, have husbands been asked by their spouses, "Do you notice something different about me?" The look offered in return is a completely baffled look. Soon, panic sets in. Is it a new outfit? A new haircut? That poor woman is just waiting for a compliment from her beloved, but her husband is too blind to change to notice what's new, even though it's right in front of his eyes.

Since we are bombarded by a constant influx of information, our brains can't absorb each piece of information with the same degree of attention. Fortunately, with RELEVANCE we have developed a number of strategies that help our clients see the changes unfolding all around them. Much like the status quo bias, this includes demonstrating value from where the project was, where it is currently, and where it is going.

Sometimes a team member may be new to an organization and doesn't possess any historical knowledge of a project. While they don't represent change blindness in a traditional sense, organizational newcomers can also benefit from being shown the past, present, and future.

Overall, change blindness is a concept that can be overcome to ensure customer satisfaction, which includes deploying version updates, something we'll discuss more in the Execute step (chapter 8). The key is to make sure there is clarity regarding what the change is, what the solution is, and most important of all, the inherent value of that change or solution.

RELEVANT SOLUTIONS PATHMAPS:
A VISUAL IS WORTH 1,000 WORDS OF VALUE

As we previously discussed in the Enhance and Visualize step in chapter 4, most people, by nature, are visual learners. Most of our customers respond better to graphics because a visual representation resonates much better than big blocks of text.

This is no different when our customers are chomping at the bit to see what solutions we can offer. After all, who really likes reading a lot of boring drivel? We create visual solution sets in part because a number of studies show that humans process images 60,000 times faster than text.[1]

In addition, over 65 percent of humans are visual learners.[2] It takes humans just one-tenth of a second for an image to resonate,[3] which is why, at Pathoras, we use our visuals in a way that highlights the most important information from the Solutions Valuations Review.

SHOWING VALUE IN THE FORM OF VALUE PROFILES PREVENTS OUR GREAT ENEMY STUCKOCATION FROM SETTING IN.

The **Relevant Solutions Pathmaps** is essentially an extension of the Solutions Valuation Review but in visual form, so our customers and stakeholders can easily digest solution benefits.

---

1 "Humans Process Visual Data Better," Thermopylae Sciences and Technology, September 15, 2014, accessed October 2019, http://www.t-sciences.com/news/humans-process-visual-data-better.

2 TJ McCue, "Why Infographics Rule," Forbes.com, January 8, 2013, accessed October 2019, https://www.forbes.com/sites/tjmccue/2013/01/08/what-is-an-infographic-and-ways-to-make-it-go-viral/#78665e037272.

3 Susan Bell, "How our brains can recognize previously unseen scenes, objects or faces in a fraction of a second," Medicalxpress.com, April 24, 2017, accessed October 2019, https://medicalxpress.com/news/2017-04-brains-previously-unseen-scenes-fraction.html.

A Relevant Solutions Pathmap shows customers where they were in the past, where they are right now and where our potential solutions will get them to in the future. We always focus on showing them value rather than simply identifying requirements. Showing value in the form of value profiles prevents our great enemy stuckocation (see chapter 5) from setting in.

As we build our visuals, we keep in mind those ill-fated irrational factors and biases that can linger during projects. This includes all of the biases we've discussed so far (including the stereotype bias, status quo bias, loss aversion, and change blindness) and employs the strategies we've discussed to overcome each particular bias.

CASE STUDY:

NEW TECHNOLOGIES, OLD PROBLEMS

Three Pathorians were serving in analytical roles for a customer of ours. As time progressed, it became apparent that the program was riddled with software tools that did not address the needs of the end users (the analysts). Tools were created that satisfied what the developers perceived to be the customer's mission need, the latest and greatest technology.

But upon working with the customer, our team of analysts discerned that the customer was unaware that the latest technology was impeding the analysts. It didn't address the true needs of the analysts, which was to identify information robustly with context behind it, as opposed to just quickly spitting out a report that mentioned the number and types of search hits. The customer had a value profile of enabling efficient resources (especially considering productivity).

Our Pathorians then created visual comparison charts of potential solutions that would address the analysts' needs and boost morale in the office. In the end, the customer chose a solution where our team acted in supporting roles as system architects and engineers to create a system that not only saved over $790,000 in labor costs to engineer the system but also resulted in significantly higher-quality analyst products.

CHAPTER 6 KEY TAKEAWAYS

Value is at the heart of every project success if it is communicated appropriately to all involved parties so everyone has a cohesive understanding of the project's benefits moving forward. If you employ tools like the Solutions Valuation Review and Relevant Solutions Pathmap and identify stakeholder value types and value profiles, you will be able to reveal solutions that support what actually matters to stakeholders. And, if you factor in phenomena such as the status quo bias, loss aversion, and change blindness, you can accurately evaluate project benefits and outcomes for the best project solutions.

- **Value types** help identify customer or stakeholder perceptions of project value in order to pinpoint how customers or stakeholders perceive project success, usually in one or both of the following value types: (1) enabling efficient resources (time, money, manpower, quality, productivity) or (2) boosting organizational morale (simplicity of comprehension, ease of communication, consumer satisfaction, team cohesion, sense of purpose).
- **Value profiles** catalog a customer's or stakeholder's project preferences by understanding the value types customized for each customer or stakeholder.
- **Solutions Valuation Reviews** are conducted to gauge the value of each solution set, based upon the value profiles that the customer and stakeholders perceive. The key is to review customer responses to the questions posed in the Enhance phase about what the client knows or likes about the envisioned project outcome, among other questions from the enhancement dialogues.

- **Loss aversion** is a cognitive bias/phenomenon where people tend to focus on a loss versus a gain, irrespective of an overall event outcome.
- **Status quo bias** is a cognitive bias/phenomenon where individuals, teams, or organizations perceive anything outside of the status quo as a loss; change is always considered a negative and is an irrational preference to one's current situation.
- **Change blindness** is a cognitive bias/phenomenon where people are so unconscious of their surroundings that real changes in their environment often go completely unnoticed.
- **Relevant Solutions Pathmaps** are visual solution sets that highlight important information from the Solutions Valuation Review and reveal such information to clients and stakeholders in a clear way (including showing project value) in order to overcome any cognitive biases that may exist among an individual, team, or organization.

CHAPTER

SEVEN

The Communicate Step: Establishing Strategic and Frequent Communication Practices That Promote Project Cohesiveness

Raw, real communication can be the most direct path to greater awareness and stronger relationships.

—Beverly L. Kaye

MAIN POINTS:

- Communication in projects is often about managing change. To successfully manage communication and change management, the value (benefit) of a project's objectives and features need to be clearly communicated to the parties affected.
- Tools such as the engagement dialogue and the **communication pathmap** (chapter 3), as well as the **Communication Pathblasts Dialogue and Tracker** and the **Relevant Solutions Pathmaps Dialogue and Tracker** (this chapter) are essential best practices

for developing, discovering, and managing how and when to communicate with certain groups.

- Strong communication effectively hinges upon an understanding and awareness of the **anchoring effect**, **signaling mechanisms**, **effort justification**, **asymmetric information**, and the **sunshine policy** (behavioral economics and psychological phenomena that affect how humans communicate).

I grew up near Albany, New York, an area teeming with Gilded Age culture and where General Electric was founded and began its legendary ascent into worldwide prominence. Albany was, in many ways, built as the result of spillover prosperity meandering northward from New York City. So, as a child, it was only natural that I wanted to soak up as much turn-of-the-century splendor as possible.

Among those iconic stories was, of course, the tale of the *Titanic*, a ship unprecedented in both its size and reputation. Today it's rare to find anyone who doesn't know about the ill-fated story—and demise—of the *Titanic*. "It crashed into an iceberg," people will say, usually with a shrug that suggests, *Duh. Everybody knows that.*

But allow me, if you will, to blow your mind. The real reason the *Titanic* plummeted to the bottom of the sea has less to do with the iceberg itself than it does with what was happening in the *Titanic*'s telegraph room. As the historical record shows, the telegraph operator on duty that night was so overwhelmed with trying to transmit passengers' telegrams (a money-producing service for the *Titanic*) that he failed to pay attention to an incoming telegram intended to warn the ship that an iceberg loomed nearby. Even more troubling was the fact that the operator never bothered to communicate that vital message to the captain.

Had the contents of that critical message been passed along, the *Titanic* might never have had such a titanic disaster. Had there been better lines of communication, it might have gone down as one of the safest and most remarkable Gilded Age innovations of its day.

A great deal can be learned from the story of the *Titanic* that relates directly to our RELEVANCE methodology. Why? Because we focus on communicating the value of a message and project solutions so that they are clear and compelling. Essentially, we want to explain why a project solution matters to you, our client.

Our communication step is designed with tools that drive strong communication practices and ensure that all our stakeholders receive solution sets that align with their particular *value profiles* (as discussed in chapter 6). Remember the *relevance gap*, which is the difference between a customer's understanding of a situation and the real value that a solution can provide. Thus, finding the best ways to communicate a solution is an extraordinarily critical step in ensuring project success and eliminating the relevance gap.

A MULTIVITAMIN FOR PROJECT SUCCESS:
USING TRACKERS TO STANDARDIZE COMMUNICATION PROCESSES

No two client situations are ever alike. That's an undeniable fact, but when you've been working on projects as long as we have, you begin to see a certain set of patterns emerge. Over the years, we've been able to create standardized processes that ensure we communicate effectively with customers and stakeholders as well as correct unhealthy communications patterns that have become ingrained in our clients' workspaces.

At the heart of our Communicate step is providing the customer with clearly defined options for solution sets, using specific tools such as our **Relevant Solutions Pathmaps Dialogue and Tracker.**

After all the work we've done to find optimal and relevant project solutions, communicating those solutions is where the rubber meets the road. Using the Relevant Solutions Pathmaps Dialogue and Tracker, we brief the primary stakeholders on the *relevant solutions pathmaps* tool we prepared in the Numerate step (chapter 6), making sure our solutions align perfectly with their values. It's a bit of a give-and-take process. We offer, and then we listen. We solicit our customer's preferred solution set, (as well as that of the other primary and secondary stakeholders) and catalog why they prefer one solution over another.

The Relevant Solutions Pathmaps Dialogue and Tracker collects information from the various stakeholders on their preferred solution set and why it may work. It allows us to see trends and why one solution may be preferred over another for the team writ large, as well as why a key stakeholder may prefer a solution different from the majority.

Why, you may ask, is such dialogue and response tracking so helpful? Because it allows us to be highly adaptable as well as to move up and down a client's hierarchy. Once the primary stakeholders have chosen their preferred solution, we revisit stakeholders who didn't get their preferred solution and go to great lengths to communicate how the chosen solution will meet their particular needs and value profile.

That's where our **Communication Pathblasts Dialogue and Tracker** comes in, which is our way of tailoring our communication blasts so that they reach the right people. We divide the stakeholders within an organization according to their value profiles and their role in an organization. We identify the value and relevancy of the solution to the stakeholders and send this information via a variety of communication channels. We also create a schedule detailing how and when we will send appropriate communication blasts to stakeholders, guaranteeing everyone will be kept in the loop.

This is important because we don't want anyone on a client's team to feel like they've been left out of the loop. Or that our communication with them is misinterpreted or confusing because they don't know us or mistakenly assume we are not working with their best interests in mind.

As far as we're concerned, *everyone* matters, whether they're primary, secondary, or tertiary stakeholders. That's why, in the communication pathblasts, we also generate communication blasts for our tertiary stakeholders which provide updates outlining *why* they need to know about the upcoming plan, *why* they need to care, and *how* it will benefit them in the long run.

Our trackers are powerful tools, not unlike multivitamins, which tailor communications and boost everyone's ability to see the same path ahead and understand why that path is the right solution for the organization as a whole. Without such a focused and highly organized set of communications procedures, the vitality of our solutions sets—and the support for those measures—may fragment and dissolve. And even worse, chaos and confusion inevitably would follow.

COMMUNICATION PACKED WITH NUTRITION:

THE IMPORTANCE OF ESTABLISHING OPEN LINES OF COMMUNICATION AND CONTINUAL FEEDBACK

Although each step within RELEVANCE identifies a particular focus (and this Communicate step is no different), we recognize the importance of communication throughout all phases of the process. Communication is as essential for project success as the air we breathe. The key is to maintain open lines of communication throughout *every* phase of a project.

That's why we're seeing activities from the different steps of RELEVANCE reemerge in this step. We use our *communication pathmap* (which we created in the Engagement step and discussed in chapter 3), as well as the *Communication Pathblasts Dialogue and Tracker,* to track our communications with every involved party.

It is a best practice at Pathoras to consistently provide status updates and feedback that aligns with our established *communication pathmap* plan.

Why does this matter so much to us and the customer and team of stakeholders we support? Because continual communication provides something called a ***signaling mechanism***, which is a signal to our customer that we care about their involvement in the process and recognize that they have control over the project. Our signaling mechanism is a means for us to show that we're merely the facilitators helping their project become a success.

We have a discrete set of practices we follow that ensures our project teams are focused on putting the best interest of our clients in place:

- We never leave our clients in limbo. The key is in the follow-up. Leaving loose ends allows imaginations to run wild, usually in a negative way. It's best to close the loop and provide status updates, or potential resolutions, for customers and stakeholders. In addition, doing so offers the added benefit of reinforcing confidence in the overall project—and in our ability to successfully deliver a strong end result.
- We avoid being too negative. We always try to find a solution to a potential obstacle. We mitigate troublesome issues. We're

there to solve our client's problems, not create new ones. So we make lemonade out of lemons, and we create a clear path out of a dense forest.

- We avoid stretching the project development time to pad our bottom line, and (through processes such as our communication pathblasts) we make sure to continually update stakeholders on our progress. With that said, there are times when it's acceptable not to meet a deadline; if this occurs, we explain why the extra time was needed and what value was derived.
- We do not assume that design, planning, and stakeholder meetings are sufficient communication channels for our customers. They're not. The client benefits far more from communicating with our project team when the value propositions of solutions are identified, (which rarely occur during stakeholder, design, and planning meetings). We've seen far too many projects use their development and requirement-gathering meetings to communicate status updates to a customer. This "muddies the waters," proves inefficient, and leaves a customer wondering about the status of a project. This is the primary reason why we ensure communication dialogues with our clients are separate from design meetings.

THANK YOU FOR THE DELAY:

WHEN EXTRA TIME PROVIDES EXTRA BENEFIT

We once had a customer who was adamant that we roll out a system for his team early. To him, an early rollout initially meant that he could include such a metric on his performance appraisal, which he thought would help him get the promotion he desired.

At Pathoras, we always want our clients to reach their maximum potential, see the benefits of their actions, and get that next-level promotion. Yet in this instance, we knew that delaying the rollout would actually benefit our client more, and likely increase his chances for that promotion he so desperately wanted.

Here's why. We explained that the system was vulnerable without the necessary security patches, which were set to debut the following week. If we delayed implementation until the new security patches were deployed, the team would then have a robust tool devoid of vulnerabilities and security risks. The delay would mitigate negative downstream repercussions and provide a better quality rollout.

The customer was grateful to know the "why" behind the delay, as well as the positive impact of our advice, and was ultimately pleased when a more secure system went into production two weeks later.

In the end, our client got a better system and his promotion. Our team couldn't have been happier for the outcome on both ends.

In any project, to ensure we stay in step with our client's scheduling needs from both project rollout and communication perspectives, the *Communication Pathblasts Tracker* allows us to provide status updates with strong context and strategic project value. This allows us to be flexible and allows our clients to set a timeline if the proposed schedule is inconvenient for their needs. We know it's critical to be respectful of a client's time while still providing frequent updates. Our tracker allows us to stay flexible based on client desires throughout the entire project's design and development process.

With that said, however, we recognize that some customers tend to be fairly "hands off" and are more comfortable with just routine status updates. Others are "information seekers" and will want to be more involved with the process. For these customers, we take additional time to determine and discuss the risks and rewards of certain requirements. The customer is always grateful for the opportunity to move a project forward according to their own particular values and risk tolerance as well as communicate on a timetable that works for them.

A COMMUNICATION PITFALL:
OVERCOMING THE ANCHORING EFFECT FOR PROJECT SUCCESS

As we prepare to communicate potential solution sets with stakeholders (typically starting with the client), we always keep in mind the perils of the **anchoring effect**, which is the tendency for people to cling to the initial information received above all else when making decisions.

In order to understand the anchoring effect, let me wander, for just a moment, into a discussion of health and fitness. Baby boomers love butter. My 65-year-old friend, for example, is so in love with butter that she calls it "liquid gold." For some people, it's practically its own food group.

Even though studies now show that too much butter is detrimental to our health, additional studies show Baby Boomers consistently overlook this warning and happily go on consuming it. Why? Because they were told early on in life that it was good for them, so they cling to that idea, even if more contemporary evidence shows otherwise. That's the anchoring effect in action.

Also think about the tooth fairy for a moment. Kids nowadays often expect a dollar—sometimes even $5 or $10—for that well-deserved loosened tooth. Some parents are in absolute disbelief at that mark-up. *Highway robbery! Inflation run amuck. They deserve 25 cents at best!* Maybe, maybe not. But the truth of the matter is that parents are so anchored by their own personal childhood experiences about what *they* received from the tooth fairy that they have trouble accepting the rewards their children expect.

At Pathoras, we never underestimate the power of the anchoring effect when we are crafting or communicating possible solution sets to our client.

Let me take this opportunity to let you in on one of our secrets. We begin to consider and mitigate the anchoring effect in multiple toolsets of the RELEVANCE steps, including the Enhance and Visualize step (chapter 4).

In that step, we specifically asked what project knowledge our clients and stakeholders were already aware of. We identified their baseline reference points so we could craft and communicate solutions in other steps of RELEVANCE, which is why we always belabor the point that information can—and will—change throughout the project. This transparency helps customers and stakeholders let go of their initial reference points and move forward based on changing conditions.

So what we're really doing in this step is providing our client with an understanding of what's happened in the past, what we're seeing in the present, and what the solution's future might be.

For example, we had a team we worked with that had been copying and pasting information into documents for years. The time they spent doing this was, sadly, absurd. We could feel their despair at how overwhelmed they felt all the time. In their current state, the team had tried to improve the process by creating a template that demonstrated where to paste information.

Yet the team was quite hesitant to try to move forward. It was, in some ways, easier to copy and paste because it is what they had always done. Though the process was painful at best, it was what they knew and were "comfortable" with.

It was only after we showed them where they had been (a total copy and paste job), where they were currently (a template), and where they could go (simple data ingestion support that would remove copy and pasting but still populate the template they had created), that the team started to be open to the prospects of a future that could be better. We had to show the value of the data ingestion and help the team to see their prosperous future to overcome the anchoring effect.

Like the above example, we provided several future state solutions that could benefit their team's productivity. The team just happened to pick the data ingestion solution after seeing the pros and cons of that solution, and several other solutions we proposed.

So, in addition to providing a "past-present-future" scenario for proposed solutions, we always also strive to provide more than one solution, with pros and cons for each, so that clients have the ability to pick the best solution that they deem to support their goals. This helps counteract a series of additional biases, including the status quo bias and change blindness described in chapter 6.

TRANSPARENCY AND INCLUSIVENESS:
THE COMMUNICATION CULTURE FOR SUCCESS

At the end of the day, open and clear communication is a prerequisite for any company that wants to claim it's a transparent organization. Customers don't appreciate ***asymmetric information***—that is, when they provide requirements and receive no information or updates in return. Asymmetric information breeds uncertainty, and uncertainty almost inevitably breeds danger. This is why, at Pathoras, we ascribe to a ***sunshine policy*** of open communication, which prevents dishonesty and conflicts of interest from arising. Supreme Court Justice Louis Brandeis described the phenomenon best back in 1913, when he wrote, "Sunlight is said to be the best of disinfectants."

ASYMMETRIC INFORMATION BREEDS UNCERTAINTY, AND UNCERTAINTY ALMOST INEVITABLY BREEDS DANGER.

At Pathoras, we believe in two-way communication and in providing information and solution sets to our customers and stakeholders in simple terms, which allows them to gain a clear grasp over a project's status and future goals on a structured, consistent basis.

We have seen far too many projects "suck in" information from their clients without providing responses back to the client (in the form of status updates, benefits of a project, expected completion of tasks, feedback from stakeholders on proposed solutions). An approach like this often leads to disaster, as the client is left to wonder what is happening with the project. At Pathoras, by contrast, we do the opposite and provide the updates our clients need (such as status updates on their requested communication schedules, project benefits, expected task completions, and stakeholder feedback, any other client-requested information). This allows everyone to know when to expect status updates and feel assured that they will receive the information they seek at appropriate intervals.

We see our clients as partners, which produces its own set of benefits. A person, team, or organization that expends effort accomplishing a task will place additional value in seeing that pursuit succeed (a phenomenon called ***effort justification***). When someone invests time in a pursuit, they want to see results. So if our customers feel like they are part of our team and openly communicate, shape the project development, and visualize the overall benefits the project will yield, the customer will truly value the project. In addition, the customer will also have a greater vested interest in seeing the effort succeed, so they are more likely to foster a team culture that's comfortable working in concert with one another.

CHAPTER 7 KEY TAKEAWAYS

At its core, the communication culture of any project should stem from the belief that the customer is your partner, not the person paying you. By including the customer in the project at intervals that are beneficial to both the customer and your team, the project turns more into a choreographed dance rather than a duel. Such strong communication steers any project (even that of titanic proportions) away from the proverbial misinterpretation icebergs.

If you employ strategic, frequent communication processes with your client, you'll have stronger relationships with everyone involved in the project. And stronger relationships then translate to project confidence—and ultimately—projects that are increasingly on time, under budget, and boost your bottom line.

- **Communication Pathblasts Dialogue and Tracker** detail how and when a project team will send communication blasts to an organization, thus dividing stakeholders within an organization according to value type, role in the organization, and value profiles. The document identifies the value and relevancy of the solution to the stakeholders while providing updates that describe *why* stakeholders need to know about an upcoming plan, *why* they need to care, and *how* it will benefit them in the long run. This allows for everyone to see the same project solution and why that solution path is right for the organization as a whole, as well as the specific needs of each party involved.

- **Relevant Solutions Pathmaps Dialogue and Tracker** track results from when a project team briefs the primary stakeholders on the *relevant solutions pathmaps* prepared in the Numerate step (chapter 6). This ensures project solutions align perfectly with stakeholder values. The customer's preferred solution set is solicited (as well as that of the other primary and secondary stakeholders) and describes why one solution is preferred over another. It is then catalogued so the project team can revisit with stakeholders who don't get their preferred solution; the project team can then communicate how the chosen solution will meet each stakeholder's particular needs and value profiles.
- **Anchoring effect** is a cognitive bias/phenomenon where people tend to cling to the initial information received above all else when making decisions. This is a phenomenon RELEVANCE works to overcome by asking what project knowledge our clients and stakeholders are already aware of. We identify client and stakeholder baseline reference points so the project team can craft and communicate strong solutions.
- **Signaling mechanism** is a phenomenon where a party signals to another a certain interest, characteristic, or quality. In RELEVANCE, strong communication serves as a signaling mechanism that the project team is invested in the client's goals.
- **Effort justification** is a phenomenon where a person, team, or organization expends effort accomplishing a task that will place additional value in seeing that pursuit succeed. This is a phenomenon RELEVANCE ensures is not overlooked by ensuring a project team openly communicates and solicits input from clients and stakeholders to maximize project success.

- **Asymmetric information** is a phenomenon that occurs when one party does not reveal information to another. This phenomenon is one that can (and does) occur easily in projects, and tools such as the Communication Pathblasts Tracker ensure communication is two-way so all parties can be on the same page and are aware of project statuses and benefits.
- **Sunshine policy** is a phenomenon that supports transparency and open communication, which helps prevent dishonesty and encourage that all parties are on the same page regarding a topic.

CHAPTER

EIGHT

The Execute Step: Committing to a Project That Delivers the Right Project Goals

To embark on the journey towards your goals and dreams requires bravery. To remain on that path requires courage. The bridge that merges the two is commitment.

—Steve Maraboli

MAIN POINTS:

- Establishing the **Master User Requirements Tracker (MURT)** and **Tailored User Requirement Tracker (TURT)** ensures strong management/stakeholder interaction, involvement, and representation at every level of a project.
- Since projects are fluid, using tools such as **MURT metrics** and **TURT survey questionnaires** provides a review of resources to ensure they've been prioritized and allocated appropriately

throughout the project. This also makes it easy to determine what a team should be doing, and when, while managing expectations at every level.

- Reformatting **gallery walks** and **user sessions** with stakeholders into lively, interactive, and focused planning meetings helps provide greater focus to a project's direction and boosts project morale.
- Additional tools such as the **Gallery Walk ToURspectives Review** or **User Session ToURspectives Review** pinpoint any overlooked requirements needed for completion before project goals are met.
- Remaining cognizant of phenomena such as the **IKEA effect** and **Not-Invented-Here syndrome** ensures project goals are not only met, but met without a bias lens.
- Conducting a **Relevance Review** and **After-Action Path Review** (at or near project culmination) ensures the project is relevant, the goals are met and exceeded, and the client and stakeholders are satisfied.

When I was in a junior in college, I asked my dad to help me build an IKEA dresser. Generous guy that he is, he agreed to lend a hand. When we began our little father-daughter furniture project, we started pulling out all the pieces and then came to the directions. "Who needs 'em?" we snorted. "*We're better than that. We got this.*" After all, my dad and I were practically IKEA experts, having cobbled together rooms full of IKEA furniture over the years.

Piece by piece, we put the dresser together, but with less success than we initially envisioned. There were places by the edges where pieces of particleboard were showing instead of the maple veneers. A tinker here, a rebuild of a section there, and—*phew!*—we finally finished. It only took us twice as long as we anticipated, but we were done. Mission accomplished.

We both took a step back and surveyed our handiwork.

The verdict? Not so good.

Our dresser looked a little crooked right out of the gate, and sure enough, within the year it was buckling to one side like it was the Leaning Tower of Pisa. The more it slanted to one side, the harder it became for us to pull out the drawers. Had we taken the time to read the directions and used the right hardware in the right places, we'd have constructed a much better finished product—one that would likely have taken a fraction of the time to build. If we had just looked at the plan in the instructions and followed it step by step, things would have looked a lot different in the end.

I couldn't prevent the memory of our little IKEA dresser adventure from popping into my mind as we began to put the Relevance Path to paper. In fact, this memory helped me shape and fine-tune RELEVANCE.

Consider where we've taken you so far in this book. Up to this point, everything we've discussed regarding RELEVANCE has primarily focused on explaining how we help our clients find the most successful and efficient project paths possible. All the previous steps of RELEVANCE that we've discussed are essentially steps toward ensuring the project is moving in the right direction. In this step, the Execute step, we get down to the business of helping clients build the highest-quality product in the most efficient ways possible.

This is the point at which the true value of RELEVANCE reveals itself. After all, it's essential to establish trusted relationships and build strong communication procedures before ever executing a plan. One of the principle reasons that so many projects fail is because everyone skips over the critical steps outlined in the other steps and wants to jump right into the execution phase.

TRY TO EXECUTE WITHOUT PROPER PLANNING AND YOU'RE HEADED TOWARD A DIFFERENT KIND OF EXECUTION ALTOGETHER.

At Pathoras, we know better. Try to execute without proper planning and you're headed toward a different kind of execution altogether. You're basically walking your project to the guillotine and setting it up for a grisly end. Which is why we learn our client's needs, obstacles, and goals early on. In this way, we can forge a strong path forward.

That's the beauty of RELEVANCE. What we're really doing is building a foolproof instruction manual, which is designed to ensure that projects don't end up like my IKEA dresser. No glaring mistakes. No leaning. No sharp edges. It's in the Execute step that we tweak that carefully outlined plan so that our clients experience optimized success at the finish line. We essentially build and ensure quality control by using the directions that were established in all the other steps of RELEVANCE.

DIRECTIONS FOR QUALITY:

NAVIGATING THE RIGHT RESOURCE AND PRIORITY PATH WITH MURT AND TURT TOOLS

So how, you might be wondering, do we move forward in this critical final phase of RELEVANCE? By helping our clients travel along the solution path that we've discussed and agreed upon with the client. Although that journey may, at times, be arduous and may require us to revisit forks in the road, by this time, we've ensured that where we're going will yield positive and relevant results.

What we do create is a workflow chart—a diagram that allows us to revisit or clarify critical needs and goals. Here's an example of RELEVANCE-related tools and a corresponding workflow process we typically use in our Execute step:

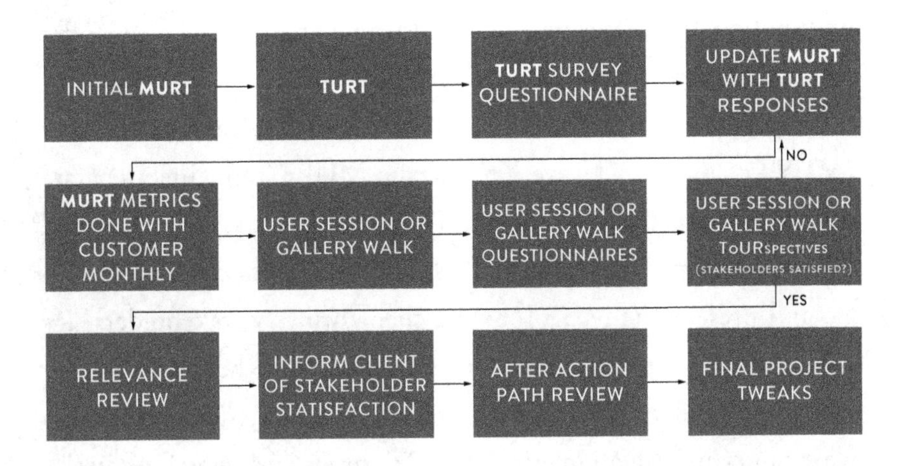

This workflow of RELEVANCE tools is flexible and shows how tools in this step can be used in a more methodical way. They can help refine project needs, obstacles, and goals as they're being built. (We'll discuss each of these tools in more detail later in this chapter.) And this workflow can work in conjunction with any other project management, change management, or IT practice. It merely adds a layer of efficiency by directly targeting and tweaking client and stakeholder needs and goals.

Almost every other step is less procedural in nature. However, we have found many of the RELEVANCE tools in the above workflow work together best in the order shown here. It allows a project team to keep in consistent communication with stakeholders and users while ensuring that all pertinent requirements, needs, and goals are being met as the project is executed.

As discussed in the Enhance and Visualize step (and really every step of RELEVANCE), it's important to be inclusive of all stakeholders, whether they're primary, secondary, or tertiary. Which is why we don't just conduct regular stakeholder meetings—and why we choose to conduct regular user/group sessions so we can obtain feedback on functionality as it is being created in the Execute phase. We offer real-time assistance for real-time projects.

This is also why we build a **Master User Requirements Tracker (MURT)**. It's also why we separate the MURT into three separate documents by stakeholder type and disseminate those as the **Tailored User Requirements Tracker (TURT)** to corresponding stakeholders and present the MURT to the client/primary stakeholders. It's critical for us to receive timely feedback as to whether the project is meeting our client's and our own team's critical needs and goals. So we conduct an evaluation using a **TURT survey and questionnaire** to collect feedback from stakeholders and report the feedback in a more quantitative form to the client. We share the metrics with the client in **MURT metrics** (at a minimum on a monthly basis) and tweak anything the client deems necessary.

Examples of MURT metrics that have proven beneficial to provide include the following:

REQUIREMENT PRIORITY %

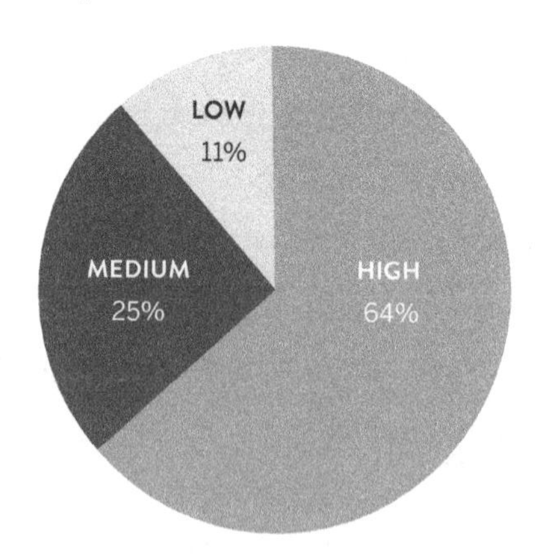

REQUIREMENTS ADDRESSING REAL NEEDS, OBSTACLES, AND GOALS, BY PRIORITY LEVEL

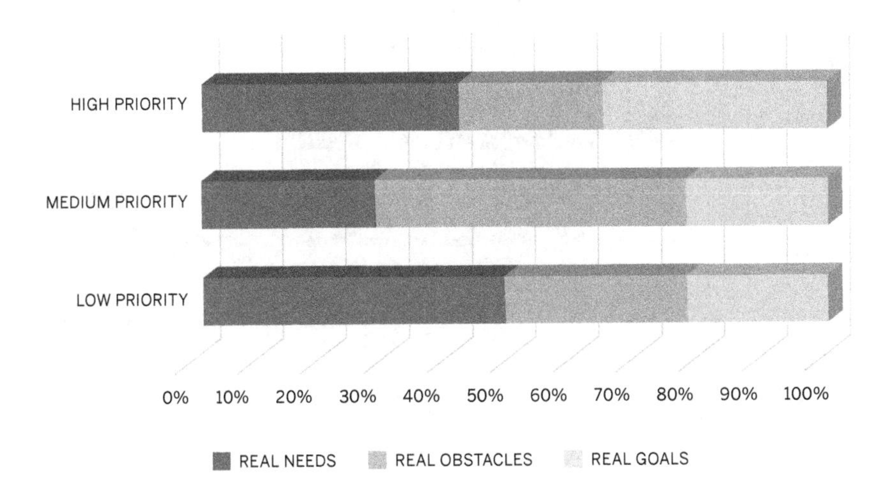

% OF REQUIREMENTS SATISFYING USER GOALS BY PRIORITY LEVEL

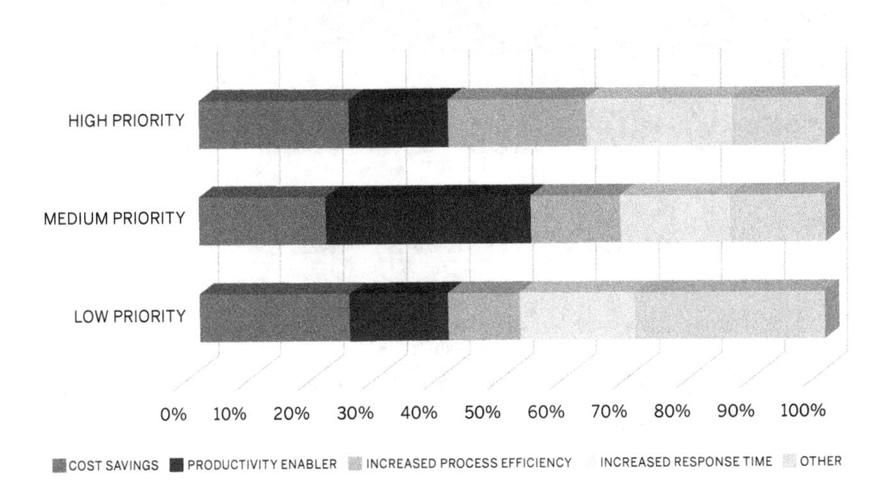

% OF REQUIREMENTS BY PRIORITY AND STATUS

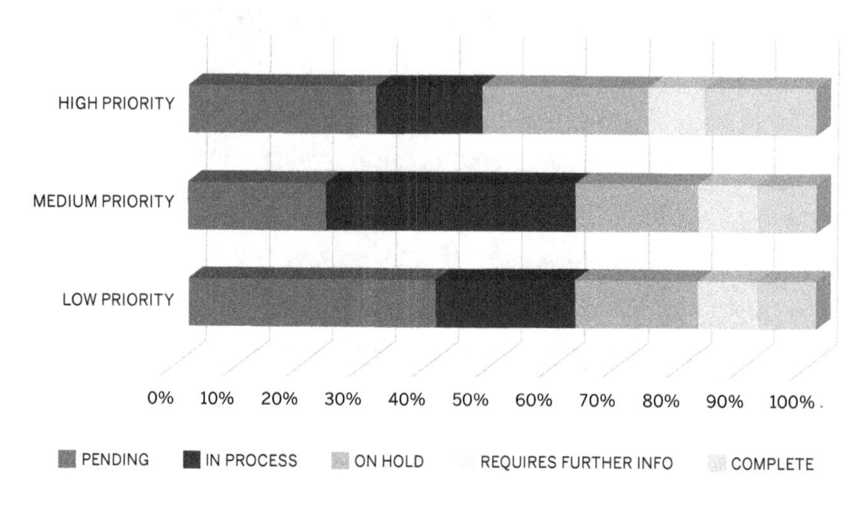

REQUIREMENTS EXPECTED TO BE COMPLETE WITHIN 30, 60, 90+ DAYS AND EXPECTED DATE REASON

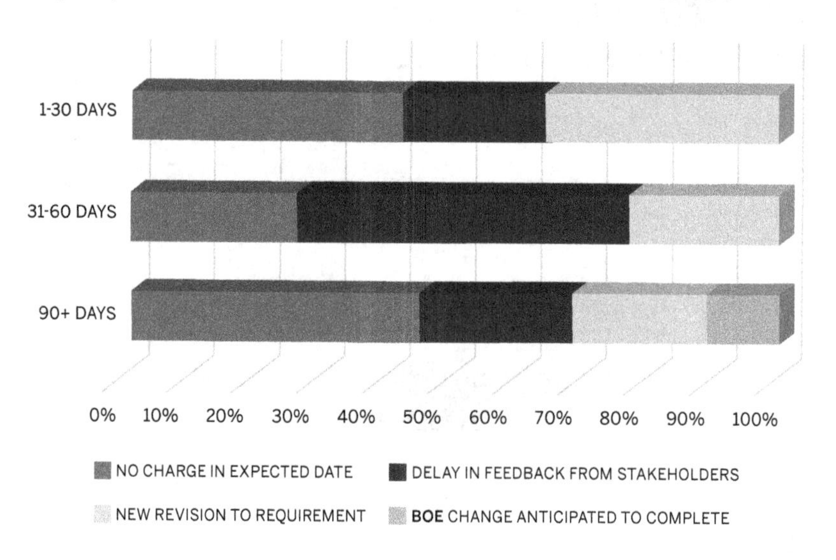

This ensures the project remains relevant, avoids any relevance gaps, and validates the project's progress to stakeholders. It also provides a concise and easily digestible breakdown of project requirements by priority status and timeline. This is done so that our clients can easily see requirement priorities and resources and ultimately track a project's progression and status as well as feel confident in the project.

GALLERY WALKS AND USER SESSION TOOLS: CONFIRMING PROJECT DIRECTION, BOOSTING STAKEHOLDER MORALE, AND SATISFYING PROJECT REQUIREMENTS

At Pathoras, we believe a project should always be a collaborative and communicative process. So a natural step (after we build a solution based upon the MURT approved by the client) is to create **gallery walks** and/or **user sessions**. Admittedly, gallery walks and user sessions are not an idea unique to Pathoras. But they're so useful that we include them in this essential step of RELEVANCE. After all, a visual really is worth a thousand words.

Here's a quick overview of what's included in a gallery walk. We create plots of screen designs, processes, workflows, layouts, and formats, basically whatever visual aids are needed to reach a project's objectives. We invite our customers, stakeholders, and end users to come in and view the plots. Similarly, we establish user sessions as lively, interactive meetings with visual aids to assist users in seeing project improvements (and offering advice on what still needs improvement).

We consider our gallery walks to be like going to a polling booth on Election Day. Every stakeholder receives Post-it notes so they can vote and offer feedback. However, unlike the anonymous Election Day, we ask that they provide their name for each comment they provide. If a stakeholder has suggestions but already sees that someone else posted the same or similar comments, we ask that they add their comments anyway.

Why? Because every vote and comment matters. Elections are decided by votes; so should our path forward be decided. We ask for names so we can contact a person if we need clarification on his/her comments. And we also have each stakeholder or user fill out a **gallery walk questionnaire** or **user session questionnaire** before leaving each, as they are tools that help us determine whether we've addressed project goals directly related to specific users or stakeholders.

This process also allows us to identify trends, which we uncover in the **Gallery Walk ToURspectives Review** or **User Sessions ToURspectives Review**. These ToURspective reviews are helpful tools, very similar to the *E-ToURspectives review* (chapter 4) and the *Q-ToURspectives review* (chapter 5).

When, for example, one user group likes one workflow, but a different set of stakeholders likes a different approach, we are able to reconvene with each group and determine why there is a difference of opinion. At the same time, we seek to develop a solution that satisfies the interests of both groups based upon their highest priorities. The number of Post-its and the changes suggested dictate whether we should stage a follow-up gallery walk or user sessions or not. If the comments require major alterations, we consider that grounds for another gallery walk or user session, which occurs after we've ironed out any kinks identified in the Post-it comments.

As we move through this process, we highlight specific places for improvement. Not only does this allow customers to divert focus away from the status quo, but it also helps clients justify the value of the project over time, demonstrating the value and importance of our project team's support to the client. This best practice has become one of the steps of process that our clients have come to rely upon, and it further solidifies trust in our team's ability to create a beneficial end product or process.

We continue with this process until our clients are completely satisfied. As each updated version is released, clients tend to feel like they're more and more involved in the project. This ultimately allows clients to witness and play an indispensable role in shaping the project's progress. Once our customer is satisfied with the solutions, we can successfully finalize the project.

MIRROR, MIRROR ON THE WALL:
REFLECTING ON PROJECT PROGRESS THROUGH THE EYE OF COGNITIVE BIAS

Mirror, Mirror, on the wall, is our project's progress the fairest of them all?

After we have mapped out our path and client concerns have been addressed, we are ready to roll out a new phase, solutions, iterations, or even our final product, right?

Not quite.

A few things need to be done before we become too complacent about finishing up the project and calling it a day. Believing that we've done all we need to do during a particular phase or in pursuit of the final product can be dangerous if we don't carefully consider the specter of cognitive biases.

Just as in every other phase of RELEVANCE, it's important for us to consider such biases. Only this time we need to judge our own progress and ourselves. Are we really seeing reality when we look at that proverbial project mirror? Which is why we conduct an internal review of our actions, something we call our **Relevance Review**.

In the Relevance Review, we force ourselves to scrutinize the merits of our work head on. We make sure we're open-minded as to how we should close the project (or a project section). We tend to ask questions of ourselves like:

- Have we met the client's success threshold? Have we met our own?
- Are we considering the IKEA effect? The Not-Invented-Here syndrome?

While building a project is often a rewarding process, there are cognitive behaviors intrinsic in the decision-making process that we are acutely aware of. There are two critical biases we need to take a second look at.

Let's revisit the IKEA dresser that my dad and I thought we "expertly" built. We literally have the **IKEA effect** to thank for that. Inspired by IKEA, the Swedish "do-it-yourself" furniture company, the IKEA effect is the tendency for humans to overvalue products that they have labored over and completed.[4] Regardless of how strongly or poorly we constructed that dresser, we placed a heightened value on it because of the work we put into it. That same principle applies to a client's projects. Though our personnel at Pathoras are adept at constructing project solutions, it's essential that we carefully assess the end product. We need to make sure we're delivering what the customer truly values.

Obviously, projects are, in many respects, "labors of love." But real success should be judged according to how positively a customer evaluates the end state. This is a best practice. We take the time to obtain constructive feedback from our customer, thus ensuring that

4 Michael I. Norton, Daniel Mochon, Dan Ariely. "The 'IKEA Effect': When Labor Leads to Love," Harvard Business School working paper 11-091, 2011, accessed October 2019, http://www.hbs.edu/faculty/Publication%20Files/11-091.pdf.

our project team has not only met the client's *success threshold* (chapter 2), but surpassed it beyond all expectations.

Then we take this self-analysis one step further by always keeping another critical phenomenon in mind: the **Not-Invented-Here (NIH) syndrome**, which occurs when organizations value the things they create internally more than items that have been created externally.

The truth of the matter is that internal solutions can be inherently inferior to external (and already produced) solutions. The Not-Invented-Here syndrome can blind people to this fact. Knowing that NIH can always crop up during projects, we're always scanning the room and staying on guard against such biases. In fact, sometimes using outside methods, codes, processes, and infrastructures will yield better long-term results than internal ones.

There are certainly instances where it is better to develop a solution internally to obtain control over a project (i.e., have the source code not be subject to licensing), but it takes a clear mind and experience to identify when an internal solution (evaluated in terms of cost, control, and overall benefits) outweighs the advantages of an external one.

If a client wants to create internal improvements, we offer our assistance so they feel ownership over the process. We also will consider off-the-shelf tools, which are neither ours nor belong to our customers. Often we have clients who will use a commercial-off-the-shelf (COTS) solution but need it tailored, configured, or customized to properly support their needs.

In all instances, the reasoning for choosing one option over another should be discussed and conveyed to the customer, thus ensuring the customer's intentions and knowledge align with a project's real needs and goals. In this way the relevance gap completely and utterly vanishes.

WHEN THE MAGIC MIRROR DOESN'T LIE:
PROJECT VALUE AND SUCCESS THROUGH THE CLIENT'S EYES

In the end, what's most important is satisfying the needs and expectations of our clients. It's the primary aim behind everything we do at Pathoras—and the reason we created RELEVANCE in the first place. This is why, in order to overcome internal bias and ensure that our magic mirror doesn't lie, we conduct an **After-Action Path Review**. This becomes our true magic mirror on the wall.

We circle back to where we started by sitting down with client stakeholders and encouraging them to share their honest appraisal of the entire process. Should anything need to be tweaked, we do so to ensure client satisfaction.

This review feedback helps us in a number of ways.

- The criticisms (whether constructive or not) reveal how successful we have been in the eyes of our clients.
- We learn from our client, so we can be better. At Pathoras, we like to say that we can always improve. We can always do better. Our humility is one of the main reasons why our clients like working with us; we're not opposed to change if it leads to improvement. After all, isn't that what projects are supposed to do? Generate change for the better?
- We want to absorb client and stakeholder criticism and work to quickly to fix it.
- We're able to continually provide clients an opportunity in the early, middle, and end stages to express their pleasure or displeasure with our progress.

- We can overcome any psychological biases we may have built up during the project.
- This is all part of our overall desire to establish an easy rapport and never let that rapport diminish.
- We ask for client feedback before the final launch to ensure our client's projects exceed expectations.
- Return business is often predicated on this step.

Recall, if you would, the 65,000 files case study we touched on at the beginning of chapter 4. After completing this project, we calculated the time and money the project saved our client.

The next page has the visual report that we provided to our client which shows that, thanks to our efforts and our on-site ***Pathorian (who supported thirty analysts), we saved our client over $2.8 million in one year in nonproductive costs. Our efforts also resulted in a contract extension.*** As a result, for the first time ever, our client was able to provide required documentation to end users and mission elements in a timely manner.

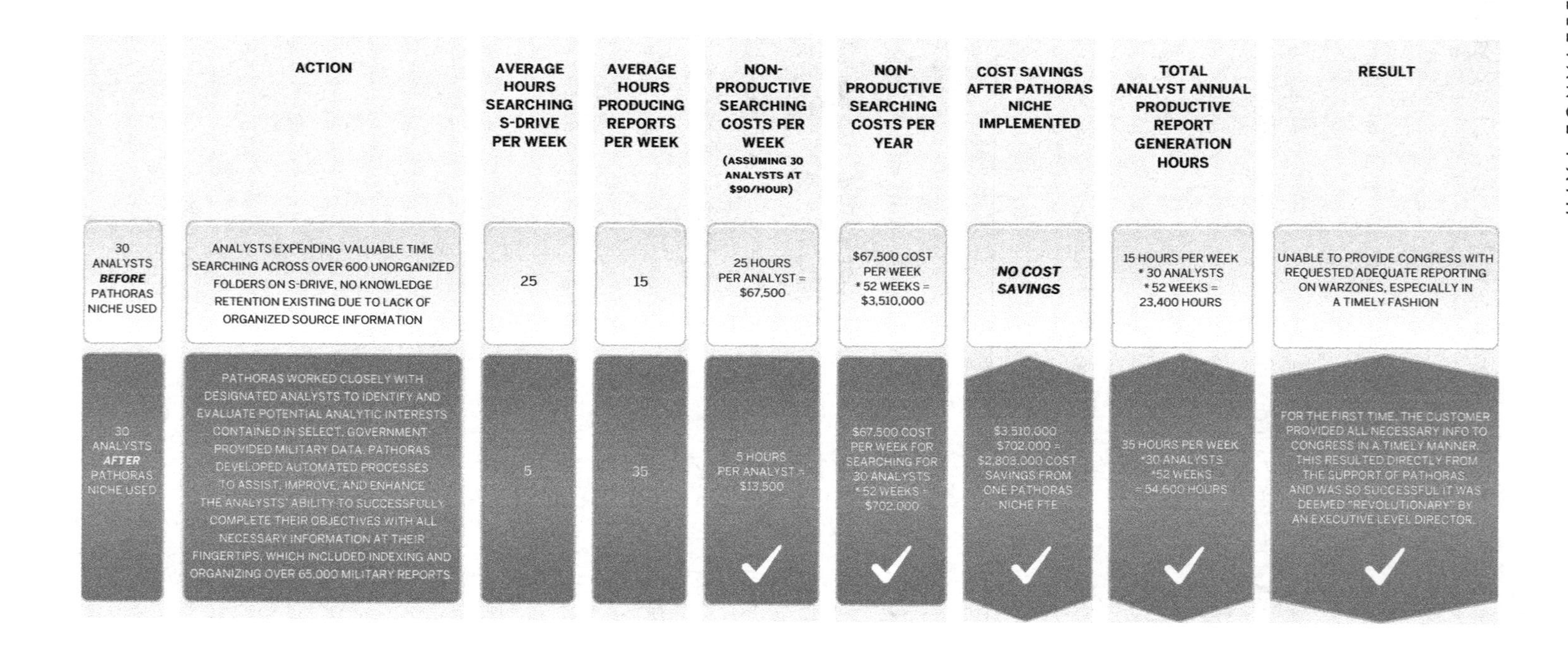

	ACTION	AVERAGE HOURS SEARCHING S-DRIVE PER WEEK	AVERAGE HOURS PRODUCING REPORTS PER WEEK	NON-PRODUCTIVE SEARCHING COSTS PER WEEK (ASSUMING 30 ANALYSTS AT $90/HOUR)	NON-PRODUCTIVE SEARCHING COSTS PER YEAR	COST SAVINGS AFTER PATHORAS NICHE IMPLEMENTED	TOTAL ANALYST ANNUAL PRODUCTIVE REPORT GENERATION HOURS	RESULT
30 ANALYSTS ***BEFORE*** PATHORAS NICHE USED	ANALYSTS EXPENDING VALUABLE TIME SEARCHING ACROSS OVER 600 UNORGANIZED FOLDERS ON S-DRIVE, NO KNOWLEDGE RETENTION EXISTING DUE TO LACK OF ORGANIZED SOURCE INFORMATION	25	15	25 HOURS PER ANALYST = $67,500	$67,500 COST PER WEEK * 52 WEEKS = $3,510,000	***NO COST SAVINGS***	15 HOURS PER WEEK * 30 ANALYSTS * 52 WEEKS = 23,400 HOURS	UNABLE TO PROVIDE CONGRESS WITH REQUESTED ADEQUATE REPORTING ON WARZONES, ESPECIALLY IN A TIMELY FASHION
30 ANALYSTS ***AFTER*** PATHORAS NICHE USED	PATHORAS WORKED CLOSELY WITH DESIGNATED ANALYSTS TO IDENTIFY AND EVALUATE POTENTIAL ANALYTIC INTERESTS CONTAINED IN SELECT, GOVERNMENT-PROVIDED MILITARY DATA. PATHORAS DEVELOPED AUTOMATED PROCESSES TO ASSIST, IMPROVE, AND ENHANCE THE ANALYSTS' ABILITY TO SUCCESSFULLY COMPLETE THEIR OBJECTIVES WITH ALL NECESSARY INFORMATION AT THEIR FINGERTIPS, WHICH INCLUDED INDEXING AND ORGANIZING OVER 65,000 MILITARY REPORTS.	5	35	5 HOURS PER ANALYST = $13,500 ✓	$67,500 COST PER WEEK FOR SEARCHING FOR 30 ANALYSTS * 52 WEEKS = $702,000 ✓	$3,510,000 - $702,000 = $2,808,000 COST SAVINGS FROM ONE PATHORAS NICHE FTE ✓	35 HOURS PER WEEK *30 ANALYSTS *52 WEEKS = 54,600 HOURS ✓	FOR THE FIRST TIME, THE CUSTOMER PROVIDED ALL NECESSARY INFO TO CONGRESS IN A TIMELY MANNER. THIS RESULTED DIRECTLY FROM THE SUPPORT OF PATHORAS, AND WAS SO SUCCESSFUL IT WAS DEEMED "REVOLUTIONARY" BY AN EXECUTIVE LEVEL DIRECTOR. ✓

We believe in always beginning and ending with the concept of value. We carefully assess how our solution addresses a particular value type. And if we can quantify that value (like we did in the above example), we can quantify how we helped our clients exceed their project goals.

Thus we close the relevance gap once and for all. Qualifying (and quantifying, if possible) value is immensely beneficial for all, as it ensures customer satisfaction and opens up the possibility of future partnerships. Our reputation speaks for itself, as does the power and utility of the Relevance Path.

CHAPTER 8 KEY TAKEAWAYS

Engaging the client and stakeholders in regular status and visual updates increases overall confidence in a project and further invests stakeholders and users in the project's success. It also allows users and stakeholders at every level of a project to be in step with the right project goals so the project can exceed expectations and ROI can soar.

- **Master User Requirements Tracker (MURT)** is a list the project team compiles, based upon an evaluation using surveys and questionnaires, to collect timely feedback and report metrics on whether the project is meeting the client and project team's critical needs and goals.
- **Tailored User Requirements Tracker (TURT)** is a version of the Master User Requirements Tracker (MURT) tailored and presented to the client and primary stakeholders to ensure the project stays relevant, avoids any relevance gaps, and validates the project's progress to the client, stakeholders, and project team. Metrics are shared with the client, and the project team tweaks any requirements or goals deemed necessary for project success.
- A **gallery walk** occurs when the project team creates plots of screen designs, processes, workflows, layouts, and formats (as well as whatever visual aids are needed to reach a project's objectives) and invites customers, stakeholders, and end users to view and comment on the plots.
- **Gallery Walk or User Sessions Trends or Unique Responses (ToURspectives) Review** is conducted by the project team (very similar to the Q-ToURspectives and E-ToURspectives reviews in the Visualize and Analyze steps of RELEVANCE) that allows the project team to identify trends (comments posted by multiple stakeholders) and unique responses that merit further review as

well as the implications of those trends and unique responses resulting from a gallery walk or user session with stakeholders.

- **Relevance Review** is an internal review to determine that no cognitive biases are present (such as the IKEA effect or Not-Invented-Here syndrome). The project team conducts this review prior to a formal project rollout. This ensures the project will exceed a customer's loftiest expectations.
- **IKEA effect** is a cognitive bias/phenomenon inspired by IKEA, the Swedish "do-it-yourself" furniture company, that shows how humans tend to overvalue products that they have labored over and completed. RELEVANCE strives to overcome this phenomenon by conducting an internal Relevance Review that ensures the project team doesn't overvalue its efforts, thus maximizing client satisfaction.
- **Not-Invented-Here (NIH) syndrome** is a cognitive bias/phenomenon where organizations tend to value objects created internally more than items that have been created externally. RELEVANCE strives to overcome this phenomenon by conducting an internal Relevance Review, thus ensuring the project team doesn't overvalue its internal project creations and to maximize client satisfaction.
- **After-Action Path Review** is conducted with the project team and client at project completion, which encourages honest client and stakeholder feedback of the entire project process. This is performed so that the project team can tweak items for customer satisfaction and ensure the project exceeds client expectations.

CONCLUSION

Translating Passion and Vision into Success with RELEVANCE

If anyone asks you what the Path is about,
It's about generosity.
It's about morality.
It's about concentration.
It's about gaining insight through
Focused self-observation.
It's about the cultivation of subjective states
Of compassion and love based on insight.
And it's about translating that compassion
And love into actions in the real world.

—Shinzen Young

At Pathoras, we understand exactly what Shinzen Young means when he talks about "translating compassion and love into action." The truth of the matter is that we love what we do. Day in and day out, we consider it an honor and privilege that our clients—truly exemplary organizations, one and all—allow us to become a part of their team and allow us to work collaboratively in meeting their goals. It takes passion and vision to succeed when working on these projects, which is why we named ourselves Pathoras, a combination of two Greek words, *pathos* (passion) and *orasi* (vision).

Through the creation of the Relevance Path, we have provided countless clients with the vision and plans needed to achieve levels of success they never thought possible. And thanks to the quality of the employees that make up our Pathoras team, we have the passion to see such complex projects through to their respective ends. In the end our recipe for success is simple: *pathos* plus *orasi* equals astounding results.

What's certain, after years and years of work, is that RELEVANCE does work. By adhering to the RELEVANCE methodology, our personnel have achieved some incredible results, including the following:

- We saved a client and his thirty analysts over $2.8 million in one year in nonproductive costs while creating a 133 percent productivity increase from 23,400 to 54,600 hours in productive analytic reporting time.
- We reduced an organization's data triage time from a fourteen-day average to just two hours, establishing real-time support to the field for a national security program.
- We saved a client over $790,000 in labor costs to engineer a series of systems that lacked integration and coordination with analyst needs, resulting in a significantly higher-quality analyst product.
- Our personnel completed a project three months early, generating more than a 72 percent increase in the total number of data fields analyzed in an audit—and "closed" an Inspector General audit recommendation that had been outstanding for over twenty years.

The benefits of RELEVANCE are expansive not only for us at Pathoras but also for our clients who have traveled down the Relevance Path with us. In short, think of RELEVANCE as being carefully designed and crafted to achieve the following:

- Establish long-term relationships among teams and organizations by engendering trust, improving communication, and identifying team workflows
- Uncover new wisdom (in the real project needs, obstacles, and goals for project success)
- Encourage technological advancement for teams that may not have been aware of processes or systems that could improve their productivity and mission
- Save time, money, and resources, while reallocating them where they're needed most
- Enable efficiencies so that teams and organizations can use their precious time to work on what really matters to them
- Help keep America safe; help clients meet and exceed critical National Security initiatives

No two projects or situations are ever the same. And the truth of the matter is that seeing things on paper is one thing; seeing them in action is another.

The best way for Pathoras to show you the power of RELEVANCE is for you to see and experience its potential yourself.

It takes the right amount of wisdom to clearly assess the reality of a given situation and even more experience to reach a relevant end state. Knowing the nuances of how to interact with customers, how to employ the right people at the right time, and how to absorb an organization's cultural dynamics: all of these intangibles are crafted into our RELEVANCE approach.

At Pathoras we crave the kinship and challenges associated with being a part of a team that's focused on high-value, high-impact results.

Which is why everything we do is built around notions of integrity and inclusivity.

Doing meaningful work is ingrained in our DNA. We've been referred to as project facilitators, doctors helping fallen projects through rehab, and even an elite "Special Forces" team sent in to clean up stalled projects.

Over the last decade, we've learned that developing strong channels of communication and relationships built upon trust can make all the difference in the world. We've learned that no matter how complex a project may be, potential success is based upon human interaction and connection as well as the ability to relate to one another on a meaningful level.

Personally, what I find to be most rewarding about my work at Pathoras is our ability to relate to our clients and their missions—and to help them achieve levels of success they never thought possible. At the end of the day, our clients are in control. We're merely facilitators to their mission success.

This book is an attempt to describe Pathoras's own path and the way we attain successful project mission RELEVANCE. Any project can meet success beyond what was initially envisioned or imagined. It just takes the right attitude, culture, and approach to get there, and RELEVANCE can help make that happen for any project.

We love hearing about teams' needs, goals, and even successes. And we love the opportunity to sit down with new clients and hear their stories.

We have a compelling desire to become—and stay—relevant and we know you do, too. Should you need our assistance we will be here, Relevance Path in hand, ready to accompany you where you need to be, where you want to go, and how you plan on staying relevant, always.

OUR SERVICES

Pathoras Corporation provides consulting services to solve problems in high priority national security missions. We combine specialized mission knowledge with deep expertise in intelligence collection, analysis, operations, information technology, and cloud-agnostic solutions to identify and solve persistent and emerging national security problems. Using a multidisciplinary approach, we quickly identify the "sweet spot" where gaps and opportunities connect, often revealing new efficiencies, cost savings, and insightful solutions.

After over a decade of intelligence and national security support, Pathoras saw a repeating pattern: (1) increases in high impact missions, (2) massive and increasing data sets, and (3) the introduction of new commercial technologies, all intended to cut backlogs, rapidly meet field requests, and save money. As technology change efforts met the cultural roadblock of mission experts, transformation devolved into "yet another tool" left unused because it lacked "**relevance**" to the mission. Pathoras's blend of mission depth, emerging technology knowledge, as well as our proprietary RELEVANCE framework proves to be just the hybrid needed to win the trust of mission leaders and IT/cloud disrupters alike, proving that mission technologies can thrive with culturally relevant analysis and integration.

Our goal is to secure the path to the future using proven methodologies and the right blend of skills and technology to solve difficult analytic, data, and operational problems.

Our capabilities include all of the following as standalone capabilities, any of the capabilities combined, or any and all of the capabilities combined with RELEVANCE:

ANALYTIC SUPPORT

- SIGINT, GEOINT, IMINT, HUMINT analysis/research
- Social media intelligence and research
- Counterterrorism, counterintelligence, cyber exploitation, countermeasures
- Open source intelligence and research
- FININT and threat finance
- Language-enabled services

MISSION SUPPORT SERVICES

- Program management
- Full-cycle training
- Requirements gathering
- Web design, graphic design
- Change management
- Business process reengineering
- Business process management

To learn more about Pathoras Corporation, please visit www.pathoras.com, as well as therelevancepath.com for specifics on the worksheets and visuals mentioned in this book.

CYBER AND TECHNICAL SUPPORT

- Cybersecurity and cyber intelligence and research
- Sensitive site exploitation (SSE)/SITEX
- Document/media exploitation (DOMEX, MEDEX)
- Technical collection, implants/proxies, triage, computer forensics
- Biometrics/identity management
- Computer network exploitation (CNE)

COMPUTING/IT SERVICES

- Data Architecting
- Data mining/shell scripting
- Data analytics, big data, automated analytics
- System integration
- System and software engineering, software development
- Cloud computing/storage (C2S)

ABOUT THE AUTHOR

Marcy Eisenberg is president and co-founder of Pathoras Corporation, a consulting and government contracting firm with over seventy employees that specializes in developing value, increasing efficiency, optimizing mission, and ensuring relevancy for customers in the National Security and commercial sectors. With her husband and co-founder Andrew Biechlin, Marcy has grown Pathoras into a multimillion dollar firm, which has twice been named to the *Inc.* 500 and *Inc.* 5000 lists, awarded one of the 50 Fastest-Growing Women-Led Private Companies in America, named an honoree of *Washington Business Journal's* Best Places to Work and *Inc.*'s Top 50 Best Small to Mid-Size Workplaces in the United States, in addition to being the recipient of the Hall of Fame Awardee for the Best of Herndon in the Business Consultants category. Marcy has supported the national security arena for nearly two decades, having served as the deputy program manager, quality assurance manager, and lead trainer for a series of projects for premier government agencies, as well as being hand-selected to serve as the team lead of a high-priority presidentially overseen program. Prior to her roles in the national security arena, Marcy served as the deputy director for a critical-infrastructure national security project at the Council on Competitiveness, an economic development think tank. For the past twenty-plus years, she has served in roles supporting federal, state, and local governments, including the House of Representatives, United States Senate, Department of Justice, and the states of Virginia and New York. Ms. Eisenberg was awarded a master's of economics from George Mason University and a bachelor's of arts in political science from the State University of New York College at Geneseo. She has leveraged her background in economics to create maximum productivity and efficiency for Pathoras and to support customers seeking low-risk, high-impact successes. It is this understanding, coupled with her knowledge and experience in meeting successful requirements gathering objectives for projects, that has enabled teams and organizations to reach levels of success beyond what they thought possible. She enjoys hiking, nutrition, fitness, writing, playing guitar and piano, dancing, gardening, and spending time with her thoughtful husband, Andy, lively sons Ryder and Skyler, and their goofy German shepherd, Badger.